spacious skies,

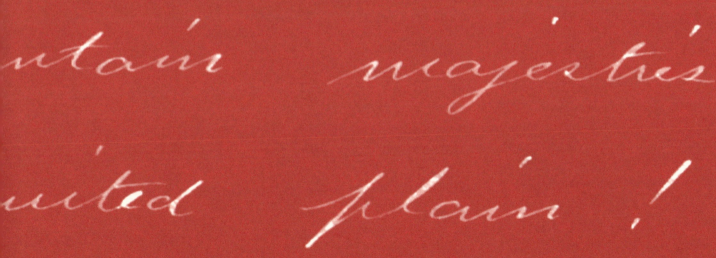

...aves of grain,

...ntain majesties

...ited plain,!

America the Beautiful

America THE Beautiful

The Stirring True Story Behind Our Nation's Favorite Song

Lynn Sherr

PUBLICAFFAIRS

New York

❧

Published in the United States by PublicAffairs,™ a member of the Perseus Books Group.

Book Design by Scott Santoro w/ Kayoko Takeo, Worksight, NYC

Library of Congress Cataloging-in-Publication Data

Sherr, Lynn

America the beautiful: the stirring true story behind our nation's favorite song/Lynn Sherr. p.cm.
ISBN 1–58648–085–5
1. Bates, Katharine Lee, 1859–1929. America the beautiful. 2. Patriotic poetry, American—
History and criticism. 3. National songs—United States—History and criticism. 4. United States—
Songs and music—History and criticism. 5. Ward, Samuel A., 1847–1903.
America the beautiful. I. Title.
PS 1077.B4 A837 2001
811'.4—dc21
2001041868

4 6 8 10 9 7 5

Contents

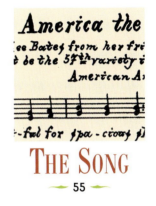

This book is for Samantha,
who made America—and the world—
more beautiful the moment
she was born.

 Introduction

This is a story about hope and dreams and the sure, undiluted patriotism of another era.

It is the real-life legend of a gifted young poet from New England who saw her country clearly from a mountaintop in Colorado and turned her vision into timeless verse. It is the unlikely tale of a modest young musician from New Jersey who conceived a melody of uncommon dignity after a splendid day at the seashore. The woman and the man never met—never even communicated—but their soaring creations so seamlessly captured the American spirit, the two would be linked forever in our national heritage.

Above all, this is a story about America.

America the Beautiful.

Why a biography of a song? Because this one gives us goosebumps. Because this one makes us proud. And because this one weaves the essence of our past and the promise of our future into a lyric of boundless optimism.

We've all sung it a thousand times, and most of us know at least the first verse by heart (although some get it wrong. One woman actually admits thinking it was, "O beautiful for spaceship guys." A third-grader who drew a picture of a jumbo jet laden with oranges, grapes, and bananas told his teacher his artwork was "the fruited plane").

It's gotten us through some of our bleakest moments: on the battlefields of World War I, after the bombing of Pearl Harbor, in the wake of the horror that a youthful president had been murdered. And it's helped salute our biggest stars: at countless commencements and inaugurals, at the World Series, anywhere there's a champion or a party. Ray Charles electrified the Super Bowl audience in 2001 with his soulful version.

When Elvis Presley crooned "amber waves of grain" at a sold-out concert, he set off a burst of teenage squeals.

It's been called a hymn, a prayer, an ode to the land, even "the national heartbeat set to music"—in short, our unofficial national anthem. In fact, numerous proposals and half a dozen bills in Congress have tried to replace "The Star-Spangled Banner" with this more singable, less militaristic, song.

I can't remember when the hairs on my own neck first started tingling, but I suspect it stems from my days at Wellesley College, where students routinely substitute "sisterhood" for "brotherhood" when singing the chorus. "America the Beautiful" was our song, because the woman who wrote the words, the poet Katharine Lee Bates, was a revered Wellesley alumna who had taught English there for decades.

But it wasn't until I started poring through the archives—a rich lode of letters, diaries, and loving tributes—that I came to appreciate Bates's talent and creativity and saw how her life spanned the great sweep of America's century of progress. Katharine Lee Bates had a childhood memory of Abraham Lincoln's assassination and a grownup's awe at the new invention called radio. At thirty-five she learned to ride a giant tricycle and admitted she was "some scared." At sixty-five she abandoned her Republican roots to vote Democrat because she believed the League of Nations offered "our one hope of peace on earth." That was just four years after women won the right to vote, a cause Katharine Lee Bates endorsed.

Her life blossomed as the nation's social conscience awakened. Bates entered Wellesley one year after it opened and spent her life educating other women. At a time of ingrained patriarchy, she was among the handful of women in the workforce, earning enough independence through her teaching and writing to travel freely and own her own house. In an age of material excess she was aligned with movements to care for the nation's poor. The public knew her as a beloved teacher and respected poet who published or edited more than forty books and encouraged young talents like Robert Frost and Amy Lowell. Privately, she worried about her weight, made up silly games to play with the children of friends, and was devoted to her dog, Hamlet, and her parrot, Polonius. Her whimsical sense of humor enlivened everything. Students were abuzz one day over the note attached to the professor's door: "Miss Bates regrets, since probably no one else will, that she will be unable to attend class today."

The contemporary newspaper and magazine articles I read attested to her celebrity and made me realize that her trip out West in the momentous summer of 1893—when she wrote the lines to "America the Beautiful"—was not just a sightseeing jaunt to Niagara Falls and the Chicago World's Fair and Pike's Peak, but a cultural reflection of the emerging power and idealism of a young nation. It was also the year that Americans invented the picture postcard, a lively new craze that graphically illustrates the self-confidence of a country on the move.

As I dug further into the history of the song, I discovered the intriguing drama behind the music, written in a moment of Victorian inspiration by Samuel Augustus Ward and elevated to new heights in our own day. Ward's role has frequently been overlooked, perhaps because so little is known about him, or perhaps because the tune's association with the words was almost accidental. But a famed classical performer recently told me he found "America the Beautiful" to be "organic. It's as if you turned over a rock and came upon the song all at once." And another modern master, Marvin Hamlisch, confirmed the unrivaled power of Ward's music through its cadence and structure.

For the first time I also understood how very American the song is. And what it really means. Why "liberating strife"? What are "alabaster cities" anyhow? And where did a woman from Cape Cod come up with "amber waves of grain"?

Finally, I found myself exploring the issue of anthems. Why does a nation need a national song? And why music in the first place? A patriot from a distant land and an earlier age concluded a discourse on independence for Scotland by noting, "I knew a very wise man that believed that if a man were permitted to make all the ballads, he need not care who should make the laws of a nation." In our own country, when the Civil War ignited a new craving for a national anthem, a thoughtful Union loyalist recognized the impulse. "Music is the universal language of emotion," he wrote. "Men will sing what they would be shamefaced to say…. It is not food for the soul, but wine."

Since one of our most enduring forms of group singing—no matter what one's spiritual belief—is the hymn, I asked the same questions of a contemporary authority. Carl P. Daw Jr., the president of the National Hymn Society, said he thought the allure of hymns was one of those left brain–right brain equations, where the logic of the text and the art of the music produce "moments of cohesion and revelation…. In a very real sense, hymns put words in people's mouths—and people are grateful for the opportunity to have their beliefs so codified and clarified." They are so memorable, he added, "that people return to them in times of crisis or doubt as a source of stability and meaning. It is also worth noting that a remembered hymn is the most portable of all religious things: No external equipment is required….[Singing] it becomes an almost sacramental experience—a moment of transcendence and timelessness, a source of comfort and strength."

Katharine Lee Bates often referred to "America the Beautiful" as "our hymn."

When I started this book and told people I was writing about "America the Beautiful," the first thing some said was "Why?" For others, it was "Wow!" But then they all paused and added the same thing: "I love that song." So do I.

Katharine Lee Bates, 1886

THE POEM

*T*he music came first, but without the poem there would be no song, so I'm going to start with the words. Some believe they were there all along, inspired thoughts ready to emerge at just the right moment. The poet herself never explained it any better.

Fitchburg Railroad

At 3 p.m. on a sunny afternoon in June 1893, Katharine Lee Bates boarded a train in Boston to embark on a remarkable journey. It was a breathless beginning. She barely made it to the Fitchburg Railroad station after packing her bags and putting the final touches on her lecture notes for the summer school courses she'd been engaged to teach in Colorado. Bates was thirty-three years old, head of the English department at the recently established Wellesley College, and this would be her first expedition out West—a welcome opportunity to supplement her modest income and take in the sights of an exuberant land hurtling toward a vibrant but uncertain future.

Katharine's birthplace

With her short, plump shape, a pince-nez balanced delicately on her nose, and hair combed back into a tidy bun, Bates hardly fit the image of an adventurous traveler. But as a colleague later wrote, "Her unwieldy body and slow movements were

in Falstaffian contrast with her agile, almost legendary wit." Katharine Lee Bates had extraordinary energy and imagination, and she would draw on both during this very significant summer.

As the train chugged westward in this last decade of the nineteenth century, it drew the young professor across an entirely new landscape, farther and farther from her Puritan roots. An eighth-generation New Englander, she was born August 12, 1859, on the Cape Cod seashore, in Falmouth, Massachusetts, which Bates would later describe as "twenty miles from any railroad, a friendly little village that practiced a neigh-borly socialism without having heard the term." When her father, a Congregationalist minister, died a month after her birth, Katie's mother took on odd jobs to sup-port her four children. But their reduced financial straits never hampered the growth of her youngest child's active mind. Katie kept a diary from the age of six, the start of a lifelong habit, early evidence of a remarkably literate child. Her first charming entries in the tiny red

Katie's childhood diary

leather notebook convey an infectious enthusiasm (with considerable room for improvement in spelling):

> The lines are to short for good rhymes. Decent rymes that is. Storys take up two many pages. So all I can do is to scribble. So I shall all over the book. Goodby, dear imaginary audience.

A later page demonstrates her budding feminism:

> Girls are a very necessary portion of creation. They are full as necessary as boys…. Sewing is always expected of girls. Why not of boys. Boys don't do much but outdore work. Girls work is most all in doors. It isn't fair.

Katie suffered no such injustice. Her grandfather had been president of Middlebury College; her mother was one of a handful of the earliest graduates of Mount Holyoke Female Seminary, the first institution of higher education for women only. So the gifted little girl who once described herself as "a shy, nearsighted child, always hiding away with a book," was afforded the opportunity to attend school.

Just before Katharine's twelfth birthday, the family moved north, to Grantville, Massachusetts (now Wellesley Hills), outside Boston, to help tend the frail health of their mother's sister. It was there that Katharine Lee Bates would attend high school. And it was there, in 1876, that she began her lifelong association with the innovative social experiment known as Wellesley College. Katharine was seventeen years old,

one of forty-three girls in the second full class admitted to the pioneering new school. With only some 11,000 women enrolled in higher education throughout the country at the time, the very idea of female college students daring to study such subjects as the Classics was still considered shocking in many circles. A Boston physician warned that "woman's brain was too delicate and fragile a thing to attempt the mastery of Greek and Latin." An influential matron of the times quoted her doctor as saying, "there will be two insane asylums and three hospitals for every woman's college."

Even the bold new Wellesley had its restrictions. There were daily prayers for the mind, daily "tramps" for the body. Lights went out at 10 p.m., and gentlemen callers were forbidden, as were cotton underwear—only silk and flannel were permitted—and candy. And while every student was expected to complete an hour of chores each day, the college spared no expense on its privileged charges. It built some of the nation's first science laboratories for women, and its literature

Student room, 1881

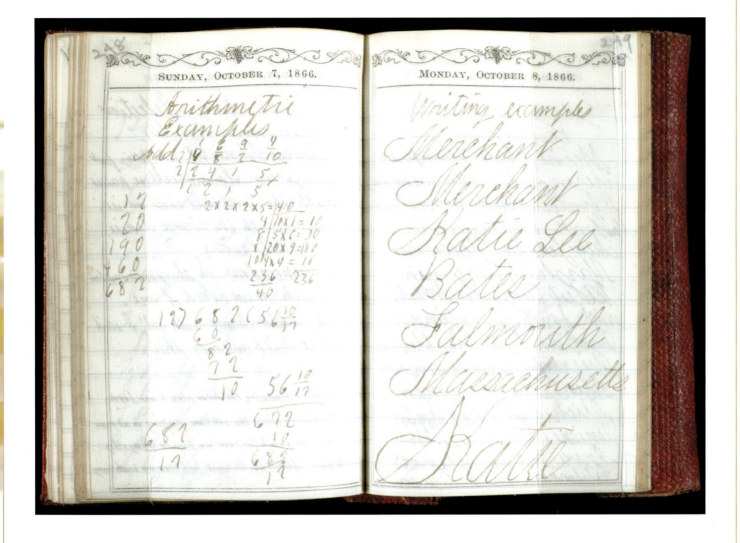

SUNDAY, OCTOBER 7, 1866.

Arithmetic
Examples

Add

$$2\begin{array}{cccc} \frac{1}{4} & \frac{5}{8} & \frac{9}{2} & \frac{4}{10} \\ \hline \frac{2}{2} & 4 & 1 & 5 \\ \hline \frac{7}{2} & 1 & 5 \end{array}$$

$2 \times 2 \times 2 \times 5 = 40$

17
20
190
460
682

$$\begin{array}{ll} 4 & 10 \times 1 = 10 \\ 8 & 5 \times 6 = 30 \\ 1 & 20 \times 9 = 180 \\ 10 & 4 \times 4 = 16 \\ \hline & 236 \quad 236 \\ \hline & 40 \end{array}$$

$12) 682 (56 \frac{10}{17}$

$\frac{60}{82}$

$\frac{72}{10}$ $56 \frac{10}{17}$

$\frac{672}{10}$

$\frac{682}{17}$ $\frac{682}{17}$

MONDAY, OCTOBER 8, 1866.

Writing example

Merchant

Merchant

Katie Lee

Bates

Falmouth

Massachusetts

Katie

department included a course in Old Icelandic. Its students ate their meals on Wedgwood china and enjoyed fine paintings and sculptures in the grand atrium of College Hall, the colossal building that served as dining hall, classroom, and dormitory. In her four years as an undergraduate, Katharine left College Hall after dark only once—on a supervised march across campus, two by two, to the conservatory, to view the rare night-blooming cereus.

But the education was superb, and "Katie from the class of '80" thrived. Like the little girl in one of her stories who vowed to "study and study and study and know and know and know," she was a dedicated student, writing more and more poems. The respected *Atlantic Monthly* published one, which earned the praise of Henry Wadsworth Longfellow.

Katie was also enthralled with the Wellesley campus, an exquisite setting of gentle hills and unspoiled

Katharine Lee Bates (3rd from right, 2nd row), 1895

College Hall, Wellesley College

valleys around a magnificent lake that would inform her sense of beauty for years to come. Founders Henry and Pauline Durant wanted not only to educate young women but to give them a sense of well-being and community, all carefully nurtured by a soothing interplay of trees, wildflowers and handsome buildings. The result was so extraordinary, a male economist was heard to grumble, "Why was not this site given to Harvard?"

After Katharine graduated in 1880, she embarked on her teaching career—first at nearby Natick High School, then at the newly opened Dana Hall preparatory school. In 1885 she was invited to join her alma mater's English department, where she would remain for forty years. By all accounts, she was an inspiring educator whose devotion to English literature thoroughly captivated her students. One pupil described "the surprising way in which she could awake knowledge one had not realized one possessed. As she talked or asked questions she seemed to tap unexpected reservoirs of information. One had never thought so clearly or to the point." The same student recalled Bates's total immersion in her work, especially when the end-of-class gong sounded: "The confusion was bewildering. There were girls rushing in every direction and everyone was talking at once.

Katharine Lee Bates, 1880, the year she graduated from Wellesley

Yet back and forth through the midst of it walked Miss Bates, reading a book, totally oblivious of everything going on about her. She might have been pacing a green forest aisle, so completely alone she seemed, as she read her book. I watched her in amazement." A colleague in the English department knew her secret: "She did not present her students with a problem to solve but with an experience to enter."

Katharine's own curiosity was boundless. During her first trip to England, in 1890–1891, she stopped to examine every flower, bird, and church she encountered in the countryside. At Oxford, where she studied for an advanced degree in English literature, she reveled in the life of a scholar. She also met the eminent professor Sir James Murray, who showed her the mammoth new book he was compiling. It would ultimately become the *Oxford English Dictionary*, but at the time, Bates wrote to her mother in awe, "*They are working on C.*"

There would be many more trips abroad, during sabbaticals and summers, back to England, to France and Spain, to Scandinavia, Switzerland, Egypt, Syria, and Italy. But she was always drawn home to her native shores, to what she called the "Land of Hope." Now, in the summer of 1893, she was on her Grand Tour of America.

The express train from Boston steamed north and west across Massachusetts, on a route that reflected the booming expansionism of the country. With the opening of the Hoosac Tunnel in 1875, an engineering triumph that took more than two decades to complete, the Berkshire Mountains no longer marked the end of the line. New Englanders had a direct outlet to what the Fitchburg Railroad's founders had called the "fertile and almost inexhaustless West." That meant new markets for business and speedy access for individual travelers like Katharine.

After a first night in the sleeping car ("models of beauty," according to the advertisements, "elegant… with every modern improvement") she woke up in New York for an early stop at the fabled Niagara Falls. Barely

Fitchburg·R·R·

To Buffalo, Suspension Bridge, Detroit, Chicago
and St. Louis, and Points West,
Northwest and Southwest.

VIA WEST SHORE ROUTE.

STATIONS.	ROUTE.	Day Express.	St. Louis Express. Daily.	Pacific Express. Daily.
BOSTON............Lv.	FITCHBURG R.R.	8.30 a.m.	3.00 p.m.	7.00 p.m.
Concord............ "	"			
Concord Junction... "	"			
Ayer Junction...... "	"	9.20 "	4.01 "	8.02 "
FITCHBURG......... "	"	9.53 "	4.28 "	8.50 "
WORCESTER........ "	"	8.15 "	3.50 "	7.25 "
Gardner............ "	"	10.26 "	5.02 "	9.13 "
ATHOL.............{Ar.	"	10.58 "	5.31 "	9.25 "
{Lv.	"	10.58 "	5.51 "	9.28 "
Miller's Falls....... "	"	11.23 "	6.19 "	10.07 "
GREENFIELD........ "	"	11.45 "	6.46 "	10.31 "
NORTH ADAMS..Ar.	"	12.50 p.m.	7.37 "	11.45 "
Williamstown...... "	B., H. T. & W. R'y.	1.11 "	8.18 "	12.06 a.m.
Mechanicville...... "	"	2.40 "	9.35 "	1.30 "
ROTTERDAM JC.... "	"	3.15 "	10.50 "	2.20 "
Utica............... "	West Shore R.R.	5.23 "	12.50 a.m.	4.50 "
Canastota.......... "	"	6.18 "		5.40 "
Syracuse........... "	"	6.05 "	2.15 "	6.25 "
Lyons.............. "	"	8.20 "		8.23 "
Rochester.......... "	"	9.35 "	4.37 "	9.35 "
BUFFALO........... "	"	11.40 p.m.	6.15 "	11.50 "
NIAGARA FALLS.... "	"	2.53 a.m.	7.10 "	12.88 p.m.
Suspension Bridge.. "	"	12.40 "	7.15 "	1.05 "
Hamilton........... "	Great Western R'y.	2.90 "	8.50 "	2.85 "
Toronto............ "	"	8.30 "	10.15 "	4.30 "
Paris............... "	"	3.30 "	9.56 "	4.12 "
London............ "	"	5.10 "	11.20 "	5.45 "
PT. HURON, Pt. Ed. Lv.	"	7.15 "	4.50 p.m.	5.20 "
DETROIT.........Ar.	"	8.45 "	1.45 p.m.	8.58 p.m.
Adrian............. "	W., St. L. & P. R.R.		3.29 "	11.32 "
Auburn Junc....... "	"		5.30 "	2.00 a.m.
Denver............. "	"		9.05 "	5.30 "
Peru............... "	"		9.29 "	7.15 "
Logansport......... "	"		10.41 "	8.35 "
Lafayette.......... "	"		11.45 "	10.00 "
Danville........... "	"		1.22 a.m.	12.05 p.m.
Decatur............ "	"		4.15 "	3.16 "
ST. LOUIS.......... "	"		8.15 "	7.30 "
DETROIT...........Lv.	Baltim. & Ohio R.R.		1.00 p.m.	9.30 "
Auburn Junc.....Ar.	"		5.20 "	2.00 a.m.
Walkerton Junc.... "	"			4.16 "
Wellsboro.......... "	"		7.61 "	6.14 "
CHICAGO........... "	"		9.42 "	7.30 "
PT. HURON, Pt. Gr. Lv.	C. & G. T. R'y.	7.05 a.m.	4.00 p.m.	7.55 p.m.
Lapeer............. Ar.	"	8.31 "	5.40 "	9.31 "
Flint............... "	"	9.06 "	6.20 "	10.10 "
Durand............ "	"	9.35 "	7.20 "	10.43 "
Lansing............ "	"	10.30 "	8.28 "	11.50 "
Battle Creek....... "	"	12.05 p.m.	10.10 "	1.25 a.m.
Cassopolis.......... "	"	1.42 "		3.19 "
South Bend........ "	"	2.28 "		4.07 "
Wellsboro.......... "	"			5.15 "
Valparaiso......... "	"	4.00 "		5.62 "
CHICAGO........... "	"	6.30 "		8.10 "

**ELEGANT PALACE SLEEPING CARS run through
without change, via West Shore Route, daily,
BOSTON to CHICAGO and ST. LOUIS.**

"The Hoosac Tunnel Route"

FAST LIMITED EXPRESS

—VIA—

❖ WEST SHORE ❖

AND

NIAGARA FALLS SHORT LINE

Leaves BOSTON daily
3.00 P.M.
arriving in CHICAGO following day
9.42 P.M.

FOR RATES OF FARE, consult the authorized Ticket Agents of the
HOOSAC TUNNEL ROUTE in your own town or city, or apply at the
COMPANY'S OFFICE,

250 WASHINGTON STREET, 250

or Depot Ticket Office, Causeway St., Boston, Mass.

HOOSAC TUNNEL ROUTE.

Fitchburg Railroad

The Picturesque Route

VIA HOOSAC TUNNEL

BETWEEN THE EAST & WEST

417—"Niagara! wonder of this western world.
And half the world beside!"
Falls. N. Y. U. S. A.

known and rarely visited a century earlier, the thunder-
ing cataract had become one of the most famous
spectacles on the continent, attracting such well-known
visitors as Mark Twain, Charles Dickens, Sarah
Bernhardt, Harriet Beecher Stowe, and the Prince of
Wales. Its lacy mists and turbulent whirlpools had been
lavishly painted and photographed, hung as prized
exhibits in the galleries of New York and London. In
1893, with some several hundred thousand visitors
each year, complaints were already being aired
about overdevelopment at the falls: tawdry souvenir
shops, dangerous high-wire acts. But that didn't
mar the young English professor's enjoyment of the
incredible show of nature. As she did so often when

Rapids above American Falls.

American Falls from Canada

Rock of Ages, Niagara.

Greeting from Niagara Falls.

moved by a moment, or an event, she wrote a poem, noting the

> Passion of plunging waters…
> Columnar mist and glistening rainbow play;
> A splendid thrill of glory and of peril.

That night, in the Line-A-Day diary that would chronicle her early life, she preserved the memory with a brief but elated notation: "The glory and the music of Niagara Falls."

It has lately been suggested that Niagara's wall of turbulent waters, then about to be harnessed for hydro-electric power, also became a cultural icon, a symbol of the can-do optimism of a nation poised to enter its second full century. That spirit moved Katharine Lee Bates as well, and it helped shape the poem that was developing in her mind.

JULY 1.

1893 Reached Chicago at noon. Beautiful Coman household.

July 1, 1893. At noon Katharine reached Chicago, for a weekend stopover at the family home of her friend and colleague Katharine Coman, professor of history and economics at Wellesley. The two Katharines, who would ultimately share a house and a life together, belonged to an elite group of female faculty members distinguished, as a younger colleague put it, by their "flashing wit, deep analysis, perfect urbanity, interest in national and international affairs, and unfailing sympathy with a just cause, or with misfortune of any kind."

Coman, known for teaching the "human side of economics," was a lifelong social activist who supported striking garment workers and founded a Boston settlement house. Bates, perennially more conservative, nonetheless was the organizing force behind the College Settlement Association, which enlisted students from the women's colleges to help poor and immigrant workers. Chicago was teeming with immigrants, and its political corruption and growing urban problems contrasted sharply with its phoenix-like rebirth after the devastating fire of 1871. The dichotomy troubled the two women, and it, too, was affecting the poem Bates would write. But for now, there was something else on the schedule. In her diary, Katharine Lee Bates called it simply "The Fair."

Officially it was the World's Columbian Exposition—a spectacular celebration (well, yes, a year late) of the 400th anniversary of the discovery of the New World by Christopher Columbus. It was an international spectacle, a giant showcase of the very best of the United States, as it was and as it would be. One entire building demonstrated the revolutionary potential of electricity, a force that had mystified and frightened

many Americans up to then ("fantastic illuminations," wrote the Chicago Herald). Another contained forty-three steam engines and 127 dynamos, roaring confirmation of the country's new raw power. The flat-out appeal to commerce and industry was balanced by elegant statues, fountains, and paintings. And the bizarre: a Liberty Bell made entirely of oranges and another fashioned of wheat, oats, and rye; a map of the United States made of pickles, and a Statue of Liberty constructed of salt. California displayed a fountain of red wine, New York a 1,500-pound chocolate Venus de Milo. Pennsylvania exhibited the real Liberty Bell. Among the 65,000 exhibits spread over 633 acres were inventions that

would change the way we eat, dress, and live. Among them: the first sliding fastener (later called a zipper), the first electric railway, the snack named Cracker Jacks, and the cereal named Shredded Wheat. Juicy Fruit chewing gum was introduced at the fair, as were carbonated soda, a moving sidewalk, and the first American picture postcards. The Pledge of Allegiance was written for the fair so that schoolchildren could participate in the dedication. Columbus Day became a national holiday.

"Sell the cookstove if necessary and come," wrote the popular novelist Hamlin Garland to his parents. "You must see this Fair." Among the 27.5 million visitors was

Helen Keller, then age thirteen, who later wrote in her autobiography, "I took in the glories of the Fair with my fingers. It was a sort of tangible kaleidoscope."

And nowhere more so than on the Midway Plaisance, the eighty-acre strip of land adjacent to the main fairgrounds that was every bit as low culture as the rest was high. The Midway, which would give its name to every carnival freak-show area that followed, was where the hucksters and the hawkers operated. Where wild animals and fire-eaters shared the bill with snake charmers. Where belly-dancers competed with the World's Congress of Beauties ("Forty Ladies from Forty Countries"). The fair's managers had conceived the Midway as an ethnological exhibit—a glimpse at the peoples of unknown worlds in an anthropological setting. Hardly. It was tawdry and demeaning to some. But it sure was popular. "It is the world in miniature," raved one visitor. "While it is of doubtful attractiveness for morality, it certainly emphasizes the value, as well as the progress, of our civilization." The magazine *The Dial* was less impressed: "Amusement, of cheap and even vulgar sorts, is being substituted for education, because most people prefer being amused to being instructed."

The fair also introduced a daring new entertainment: a 26-story, 1,200-ton steel structure that took passengers on a ride around a circle. The inventor was an engineer from Pittsburgh named George Washington Gale Ferris, who had simply, uniquely reinvented the wheel. During the six months that the fair was open, 1.5 million visitors paid fifty cents apiece for the twenty-minute ride on the Ferris wheel: two revolutions around, with six stops, in wood-paneled cars with plush uphol-stery and glass windows. The carriages held sixty passengers each and were the size of train cars; the view was the highest in the fair. Surely Mr. Ferris's elaborate new toy surpassed the intricate tower produced by M. Eiffel at the Paris fair four years earlier.

And that was the point: to show the world that America could do it better, or at least as well, as the European model on which the country had been founded. The New World was on its own now, staking its prestige on the power on display—artistic, commercial, technological—as the nation charged into the twentieth century. The president of the United States elaborated on opening day.

Just after noon on May 1, 1893, surrounded by a quarter-million men in bowler hats and women in long dresses, President Grover Cleveland spoke with pride of the American "enterprise and activity " before him. "We stand today in the presence of the oldest nations of the world," he said, "and point to the great achievements we here exhibit, asking no allowance on the score of youth. …I cherish the thought that America stands on the threshold of a great awakening. The impulse with which this Phantom City could rise in our midst is proof that the spirit is with us." He went on to laud the nation's "unparalleled advancement and wonderful accomplishments." And then he said, "As by a touch the machinery that gives life to this vast Exposition is now set in motion, so at the same instant let our hopes and aspirations awaken forces which in all time to come shall influence the dignity, and the freedom of mankind."

With that, President Cleveland pressed his finger on a gilded lever, firing up an electrical charge that

The Ferris wheel

Grover Cleveland at the opening day ceremonies, World's Columbian Exposition

switched on a thunder of machinery. Simultaneously, a mammoth U.S. flag was unfurled, and as the wind whipped it open, the banners of other nations fluttered free, officials of some fifty foreign countries roaring their approval. The chorus was supported by the spray of fountains shooting water one hundred feet into the air, accompanied by the thunder of guns in the harbor, along with steam whistles and far-off bells. As the orchestra struck up the song already known as "America"

("My country 'tis of thee"), some 10,000 voices joined in. The World's Fair was officially open.

Its centerpiece was an architectural Utopia conceived as a model city of the future: fourteen carefully coordinated buildings around a central court of honor, all constructed in the European Beaux-Arts style and finished with a stucco-like exterior that looked

View of the White City from the roof of the Manufacturers & Liberal
Arts Building, World's Columbian Exposition

like marble and was painted bright white. The effect was dazzling, especially at night when thousands of incandescent light bulbs made it glow. The White City of Chicago became the impetus for decades of urban beautification around the nation. It would also leave an indelible impression on Katharine Lee Bates, another stone in the mosaic of impressions from her journey. One verse of a poem she wrote on the spot concluded,

> All men were poets for one brief, bright space
> In the White City.

Late in the afternoon of July 3, she and Katharine Coman boarded a train for their summer classes in Colorado. Bates took out her diary and wrote of the fair, "A thing of beauty."

"A Kansas Wheat Field."

and what they stood for, unleashed in her a "quickened and deepened sense of America." Her diary entry reveals her unabashed love of country: "A better American for such a Fourth." The poem was almost ready.

On Wednesday, July 5, Bates arrived at Colorado Springs and settled in for the three-week summer session at nearby Colorado College. The town, just over two decades old with only 13,000 inhabitants, had been founded as a genteel resort by railroad tycoon William Jackson Palmer. He was particularly taken by its setting on the high plains, its dry air and its mineral springs, all in the shadow of Pikes Peak ("only twelve miles distant, and seemingly not more than three," according to the college prospectus). The mountain also gave its name to the town's main street, Pikes Peak Avenue, which

JULY 3.
— Work at those!

1893 The Fair. "A thing of beauty." Off again at 5 P. M.
Fourth of July.

Tuesday was Independence Day, and Katharine Lee Bates found patriotic significance in the rich view out her window: field after field of Kansas wheat, glowing in the golden summer sun and swaying in the hot July wind. She later wrote that the exhilarating vistas,

JULY 4.

Fourth of July.
"A better American for such a Fourth.
Hot sirocco run across western Kansas.
1893 Fertile prairie. Dropped Katharine and mother at Emporia.

Colorado College

A noted Shakespearean scholar had come from Harvard, an astronomer from Amherst. Katharine Coman would teach "The Industrial History of England" (and sell her book on the subject). Katharine Lee Bates would teach two courses, one on Chaucer and one that included Latin passion plays, an oddity not lost on the very perceptive Miss Bates: "My own subject, which seemed incongruous enough under that new and glowing sky, was English Religious Drama."

In her free time, Katharine and the others enjoyed a round of tourism that left her gasping for adjectives. She took in the area's canyons and lakes and glens, its stunning red-rock boulders, "all so marvelous that our stock of exclamations gave out." One night while the moon was bright, she visited the Garden of the Gods and heard a howling coyote.

dead-ended into another Palmer creation: the turreted Victorian structure known as The Antlers, an imposing luxury hotel that promised its guests an unusual two bathrooms on each floor. This would be Bates's summer address—a civilized oasis in the middle of gold-rush country that stunned her "New England eyes." She was particularly taken with the "purple range of the Rockies," so sublime, they "smote my pencil with despair." But not for long.

The school, too, was a novel experience, its simple buildings on the treeless plain a far cry from the country estate that shaped Wellesley. The president of Colorado College had imported his summer faculty from the East to put his students of the West "in contact with the brightest minds and most progressive spirits of the country." It was an impressive group. The president of Brown University was there to lecture on the Silver Question, a topic so hot in this mining center that an audience was expected from around the state.

K-7 St. Peter's Dome, Short Line Railway, Colorado.

116. Gateway to the Garden of the Gods, Colo.

124. Cathedral Spires, Garden of the Gods, Colo.

Top: Garden of the Gods; Bottom: Cathedral Spires

One afternoon she traveled to the mining town of Cripple Creek over five miles of terrible roads. A cave-in forced her to spend the night with no baggage but a volume of Browning. It was, she decided, "an enchanted summer."

But the crowning moment—what Katharine Lee Bates later called the "supreme day of our Colorado sojourn"—came toward the end of the session, when the visiting teachers were invited on an excursion to the top of the mountain that towered over the town. It was an irresistible magnet for travelers and tourists alike. Admired for centuries by Native Americans, then Spanish explorers, it took its name from the young army officer who sighted it in 1806, Zebulon Montgomery Pike.

At 14,110 feet, Pike's Peak was not the tallest of the Rockies, nor was it the most daunting. True, Lt. Pike and his men had been turned back in their ascent by heavy snows, and he is said to have predicted it would never be conquered. But by midcentury a succession of mountaineers had carved a trail to the summit, and in 1858 the first white woman, Julia Holmes, climbed the peak, wearing bloomers and Indian moccasins.

What made Pikes Peak so enticing was its location: smack on the edge of the Great Plains, the first grand feature a prospector or sod-buster or any settler would see on the way to the Golden West. They painted its name on their wagons as a symbol of Yankee determination—"Pikes Peak or Bust!" And though more than a few returned East with "Busted" scrawled over their hopes, the glory of the peak with the snow glistening on its cap never dimmed.

On Saturday, July 22, 1893, Katharine Lee Bates got her chance to meet the famous mountain. The cog railway that had been opened a few years earlier wasn't operating that day, so the professors piled into a horse-drawn wagon with the pioneers' slogan emblazoned on its tailboard. At first the twisting path took them upward through thick pines and brilliant wildflowers, a dazzling landscape, but after they reached the halfway house and exchanged their horses for sturdy mules, the scenery changed dramatically. As they bumped long the narrow carriage road, with its perilous turns and precipitous dropoffs, the woods were replaced by "a waste of dead white stems, a ghostly forest." Huge boulders and dusty rocks threatened every step. The journey took hours, and the merry party grew hungry, but when an astronomer in their midst warned them of the danger of altitude sickness, the lunch baskets went untouched.

As they reached the Gate-of-Heaven summit—nearly three miles high in the clear crystal air, above the clouds and beneath radiant blue heavens—Katharine fell silent. Regrettably, two members of their party

Campers on their way to Pike's Peak or Bust!

The Carriage Route to Pike's Peak

took ill and fainted, cutting short their stay at the top. But for Katharine Lee Bates her "one ecstatic gaze" at the panoramic view across the vast continent was a revelation. To the east, the golden sweep of plains across America's heartland; to the west, the regal mountains that outlined the pioneers' dreams. All the images and impressions she had been collecting on her journey coalesced in the infinite horizons before her. America's possibilities were limitless. That night when she returned to the Antlers Hotel, she wrote in her diary,

"Most glorious scenery I ever beheld." More significantly, she opened her notebook and jotted down some verses that had come to her on the spot: "*O beautiful for...*"

Here is her own recollection:

It was then and there, as I was looking out over the sea-like expanse of fertile country spreading away so far under those ample skies, that the opening lines of the hymn floated into my mind.

WEST FROM SUMMIT OF PIKE'S PEAK.

The view from the summit, as Katharine Lee Bates likely saw it

JULY 22.

1893 "Pike's Peak or Bust!" Most glorious scenery I ever beheld.

Katharine's telegram. The operator misspelled her mother's name ("Bath") but it got there anyway.

No matter how many times she told the story, Bates always invoked the same mystical, almost divine imagery: The words of the poem "sprang into being"; they were "promoted in my mind"; they "floated" into her consciousness. There was even a certain sense of destiny in the way she referred to the "notebook that was traveling with me." Never did she take credit for sitting down and thinking the lines up or writing them all down. Nor did she suspect the impact the words would have on the world around her. She knew the moment was meaningful, because she dashed off a telegram to her mother from the peak. "Greetings from Pikes Peak glorious dizzy wish you were here," it read. But the poem was set aside.

Ten days later, Katharine Lee Bates and Katharine Coman left Colorado Springs for the journey home, stopping one night in Denver, then crossing Nebraska and Iowa on the way to Chicago. This time they stayed for nearly a week, visiting Jane Addams's Hull House, the model for the settlement houses around the nation, and spending three full days at the World's Fair. They went to the Woman's Pavilion, the first American exhibit of women's achievements in a building designed by a female architect, Sophia Hayden, a rousing display that no doubt reinforced the determination of "the Professors Katharine." They also signed their names in the Wellesley guest book, took in Buffalo Bill's famed Wild West Show, and rode on the Ferris wheel.

On August 9, Katharine Lee Bates headed home, arriving the next day in time for tea. She spent her first days back at Wellesley unpacking, answering the mail that had piled up, and "relating [the] history of my wanderings." All the while, her new poem languished in her notebook. The diary entry for August 15 explains why the public wouldn't see it for another two years: "Consider my verses. Disheartening."

5 ——   **AUGUST 15.**   *Clara's Birthday.*

189 3. Into Boston with mother. Consider my verses. Disheartening.

Samuel Augustus Ward, left, with a friend, Samuel Jacobus

THE MUSIC

Now, *the other star of this drama. The story of the music has rarely been told, no doubt because the record is infuriatingly sparse. So here is the fullest account available, everything I could learn about the origin of the stately score.*

Five years before Katharine Lee Bates conceived her poem atop Pikes Peak, an ancient verse appeared in print with a brand new melody. The plaintive hymn, "O Mother, Dear Jerusalem," was derived from sacred Biblical texts and first adapted into English around 1600 by a Scottish clergyman named David Dickson. Its stirring new music was composed by Samuel Augustus Ward, a Victorian gentleman who served as the organist at Grace Episcopal Church in Newark, New Jersey.

A descendant of Newark's Revolutionary-era founders, Ward was born December 28, 1848, and attended local public schools in a city fast becoming a major manufacturing center. He was a "natural-born musician," in the words of a contemporary, and took up the accordion at the age of six while recovering from a broken leg. When his father, a shoemaker, had a similar accident some years later, Sam left school to help support the family. By the time he was a teenager, he was giving piano lessons to local students. He also played the organ, so skillfully that he was hired at sixteen as a church organist in Manhattan. Although he had no formal music training, he studied

Broad Street, Newark, N.J., 1892

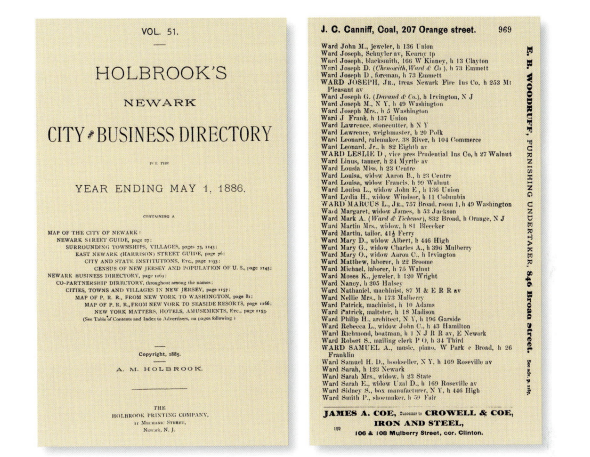

Newark City Directory, 1886

under a number of teachers in New York City and in Newark. With his own pupils, he was a stickler for the basics. "You mustn't play it that way," he cautioned one of his daughters who had picked up piano on her own. "Listen to Papa and don't play the music by ear. Learn to read what the composer wrote. You'll never be a true musician unless you know harmony."

Self-confident and self-made, Sam Ward also displayed an admirable business sense. He opened a store that sold pianos, organs, and sheet music—a thriving Newark emporium that outgrew three separate locations. And he composed music, always drawing his own staffs on a clean sheet of paper.

At age thirty-two, Ward joined Grace Church, an imposing fortress of local brownstone in the heart of the thriving city, where he played the organ for much of Newark society. But his real talent lay in the human voice, and on a trip to Europe he heard choir after choir

Grace Episcopal Church, Newark

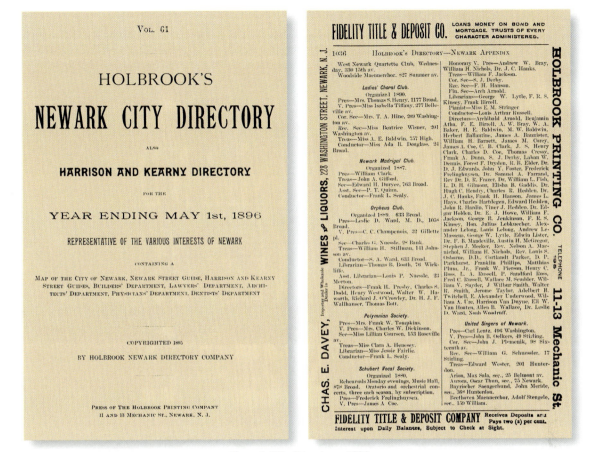

Newark City Directory, 1896

in the great cathedrals of the Continent. Back home his passion for choral works intensified. One night he invited a number of men with fine voices to his home for a round of singing. The evening proved so satisfying in those days before electronic entertainment that the group became formalized as the Orpheus Society. Some months later, in 1889, the chorus gave its first public performance, inaugurating a yearly chain of sought-after public concerts that remains unbroken today. The

conductor for the first fourteen years was Sam Ward.

By all accounts, the short, stocky Ward was an energizing force. "He could make a men's chorus sing, and at times seemed to electrify his singers," said a colleague. The audiences responded with tumultuous applause; the chorus, with awe. "The fifty human pipes of Orpheus recognized the hand of a master," said one member of the chorus, in the opulent language of turn-of-the-century America. "The singers themselves have

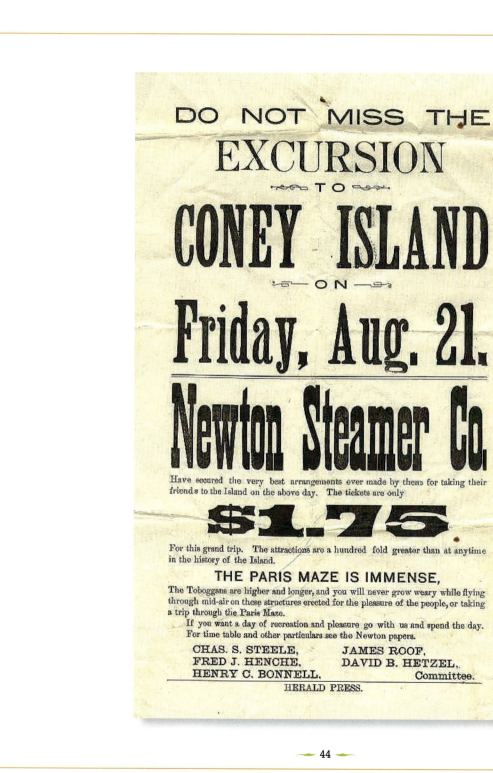

DO NOT MISS THE

EXCURSION

TO

CONEY ISLAND

ON

Friday, Aug. 21.

Newton Steamer Co.

Have secured the very best arrangements ever made by them for taking their friends to the Island on the above day. The tickets are only

$1.75

For this grand trip. The attractions are a hundred fold greater than at anytime in the history of the Island.

THE PARIS MAZE IS IMMENSE,

The Toboggans are higher and longer, and you will never grow weary while flying through mid-air on these structures erected for the pleasure of the people, or taking a trip through the Paris Maze.

If you want a day of recreation and pleasure go with us and spend the day. For time table and other particulars see the Newton papers.

CHAS. S. STEELE,   JAMES ROOF.
FRED J. HENCHE,   DAVID B. HETZEL,
HENRY C. BONNELL,   Committee.

HERALD PRESS.

stood in wonder at the sonorous outpouring to which they were lending a single voice." He found the conductor "sanguine in temperament, learned in the art of music, compelling attention and exacting obedience." Rehearsals, he continued, engendered "a certain fear and trembling" among the singers, who marveled "that the little man before them should have such power." To an Orpheus baritone, Ward's dictatorship was benevolent: "Those of us who knew him well always spoke of him as Sam Ward, but invariably we addressed him as Mr. Ward. There was a quiet dignity about him that made people courteous at all times…. At concerts his words were 'Watch me, gentlemen.' Needless to say, it was a command duly heeded."

Sam was also an artistic soul, with a special fondness for the novels of Dickens and the poetry of Tennyson and Longfellow. In 1871 he married Virginia Ward (no relation), the daughter of a Civil War general, and startled her by bringing a landscape painting to their new and unfurnished home. "We can get along without a lot of furniture," he told her, "but we have to have art."

The couple had four daughters, only two of whom survived. Their heirs, and his chorus, might be the only ones to remember Sam Ward today if it hadn't been for the day trip he made to Coney Island—one that rivals the journey Katharine Lee Bates made to Colorado in patriotic consequence.

According to the story handed down by his family, Sam and his friend Harry Martin—and possibly Virginia as well—went to the beach resort on a glorious summer day in 1882. Sam was thirty-three, the same age

as Katharine Lee Bates when she traveled to Colorado. And his destination, like Pike's Peak, had already earned its place in the pantheon of American tourism.

An established getaway for the elite of Manhattan, Coney Island also served middle-class day-trippers from the surrounding area. It was a sandy playground in Brooklyn, a carefree place to escape the sweltering city heat. "If Paris is France, then Coney Island, between June and September, is the world," boasted a local developer. And you could get there easily by carriage, by train, or on the steamboat from Manhattan ($1 round-trip) or directly from Newark. That's how Sam Ward took his auspicious trip.

The sea route, according to *Scientific American*, was the best way to approach Coney Island because "then, and then only, can the beauty of this ephemeral Venice be appreciated." A popular author described his own such excursion several years later, "a rare trip down the bay in sunny summer weather, with just enough breeze to make everybody happy. Children romped up and down the upper decks, and women in fresh, cool summer wear found comfort in camp-chairs. …Big steamers, little tugs, handsome yachts, and white-sailed vessels all were of interest on a day like that, with the special attraction of a great ocean liner sweeping grandly out to sea, leaving its long drifting banner of smoke behind. Then the Island rose up out of the sea— a horizon of towers, domes, spidery elevations, and huge revolving wheels."

Of course, the famous roller coaster hadn't been built when Sam Ward took his trip, nor had the popular steeplechase. And the legacy of the Chicago World's Fair

Steamer to Coney Island

Greater New York Souvenir

Coney Island.

COPYRIGHT, 1897, BY ERNS

Old Pier.

BATHING AT CONEY ISLAND.

2052   THE IRON PIER. Coney Island. N. Y.   ILL. POST CARD CO., N. Y.

had yet to materialize: a Ferris wheel, the freak show, the carnival on the midway. It would be another two decades before the crowds got so thick that some 200,000 postcards would be mailed from Coney Island in a single day. But the big hotels sat grandly on the beach, and the clams and the bands and the boardwalk beckoned. So while we don't know for sure how Sam and Harry (and perhaps Virginia) spent the day, they had plenty of options.

It could be that once their boat docked on the Iron Pier, they took a locker and enjoyed the wide swath of beach on the Atlantic Ocean. Perhaps they lunched on a hot dog, Coney Island's trademark food, or listened to oompah music at one of the beer gardens. Maybe they rode the steam elevator to the top of the Iron Tower, a thrilling souvenir from the 1876 Philadelphia Centennial Exposition that afforded a bird's-eye view of the grounds. What we do know is that at some point—on this trip, or perhaps on an earlier one—Sam Ward, sporting a dashing handlebar mustache, posed with his pretty wife Virginia for a local photographer, who memorialized their outing on a tiny tintype.

The rest is musical history.

On the journey home, Sam and Harry stood at the rail of the graceful sidewheeler steaming back to the city. A soft puff of air stirred the waves as seagulls wheeled overhead. On board, a two-piece orchestra entertained the travelers. Suddenly, Sam began to hum a tune. Here is how the next part of the story was recounted to a reporter by his son-in-law more than half a century later:

"Harry," he said to his friend, "if I had something to write on, I'd put down a tune that has just come to me."

Harry dug in his pockets. He fumbled through his coat, his trousers, his vest, searching for some paper. Finding none, he took off a starched linen cuff and gave it to his friend who, leaning on the boat rail, drew a staff and clef and wrote the melody of *America the Beautiful*.

Apocryphal? Maybe. But who's to say that an amusement park and an ocean are any less inspirational than a World's Fair and a mountain?

Of course, "America the Beautiful" did not exist in 1882. The tune Sam Ward wrote after that day at the beach was a new setting for the hymn "O Mother Dear Jerusalem," which already enjoyed a lengthy and hallowed musical history. According to the chronicles,

> It was sung by the martyrs of Scotland…. It has rung in triumphant tones through the arches of mighty cathedrals; it has been chaunted by the lips of kings, and queens, and nobles; it has ascended in the still air above the cottage roofs of the poor…on every continent, by every seashore, in hall and hovel.

Now it rang out from Sam Ward's organ at Grace Episcopal Church in Newark, for its first public performance by a chorus of two hundred men and boys, very likely under the baton of Harry Martin, who served as

Samuel and Virginia Ward

Grace Church as Sam Ward knew it

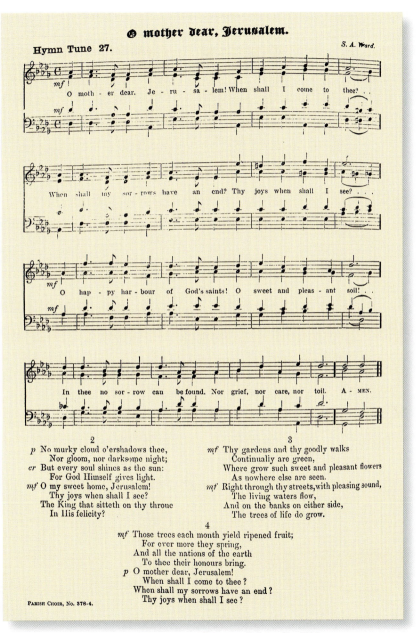

The first publication of "Materna," July 12, 1888

choirmaster at the church. The only eyewitness account that survives comes from a member of the chorus, whose description of the debut reinforces the image of the composer as a careful disciplinarian. "Some of us had manuscripts and some printed single sheet copies, which we were asked to leave in the choir room," he remembered, "and as Sam asked this, I have no doubt it was done."

Ward called his new tune "Materna"—reportedly in sorrow for the death of his young daughter Clara, named for the wife of Ward's idol, Robert Schumann; or perhaps it was in keeping with the mournful sentiment of the hymn. Six years later, on July 12, 1888, it was published in *The Parish Choir*, a five-cent weekly that made new works available to eager congregations. Shortly afterward it turned up in the Episcopal Hymnal and then found its way into the hymn books of other denominations as well.

Meanwhile, Samuel Augustus Ward composed other hymns, "melodious and eminently singable," according to an employee at his store. Perfectly acceptable to my ears, I should add. But only "Materna," with its simple nobility, endures. One of the men who succeeded Ward told me why. "Anybody can sit down and write a hymn tune, but this one is most remarkable," explained James MacGregor, the organist at Grace Church for the past forty years. "The melodic profile just stands alone. You have to be an interesting character to write a daring line like that." He also pointed out a neat touch in the four-part harmony that is evident in the original score: The first line of the soprano melody is repeated on the third line of the bass part. "I've never seen that anywhere else. The harmony is a bit primitive, but not a note should be changed. It's perfect."

The composer himself seems to have agreed. One day in the late 1890s he was strolling through downtown Newark when he heard the singing of children's voices through an open window. As he stopped he recognized the music as his own. When Sam got home he reported the incident to his family, displaying a candor unusual for such an unassuming fellow. "I stood and listened until they finished it," he said. "I never realized until I heard those dear little children singing it how beautiful my melody is. It was a very moving experience."

And it is a tantalizing indication that Sam Ward might have divined the far grander audience about to embrace his melody born on the sea.

THE SONG

 *ime now for the planets to line up. If they hadn't—if the parallel lives of Sam Ward and Katharine Lee Bates had never intersected—we'd be singing a very different tune. Lucky for us, a song was born.*

Marvin Hamlisch was sitting at the piano, demonstrating with gusto why the music to "America the Beautiful" works so well. "It's simple and sweet," said the composer of *A Chorus Line* and an array of other Broadway and Hollywood megahits, running his fingers across the keys. Then he slid into the refrain, raising his voice with the high notes and belting out the words like a kid in the choir: "*A-MER-i…*" Mid-syllable he stopped and turned to me excitedly. "It's that climb up, that jump to '*America!*' that gives you a feeling

Katharine Lee Bates, 1895

of reaching for something big. If this song were not about America, that's where you'd say, *'I love you!'* That's where you'd say *'I need you!'* That's where you'd say, *'I can do this!'"* Actually, he sang those words. Hamlisch leaned forward and played the four big notes again—*dah DUH dah dah*—twice, this time completing the line: "*A-MER-i-ca! A-MER-i-ca!*" He paused and let his fingers retrace the soft melody of the opening verse, the part that ends with "*the fruited plain.*" "It's very relaxed up to that point," he mused, putting it all together, "and then it just bursts forward."

He could have been describing the story behind the song.

Sometime in the year after she returned from Colorado, Katharine Lee Bates reconsidered the verses in what she called her "scrubby" little notebook. Already a published author, she apparently asked a friend to help place the poem she then called "America." The chain of events is nowhere acknowledged in her own accounts—in fact, she claimed nothing happened until 1895. But a letter I found in her files reveals that while traveling in England in 1894, she learned the poem had been accepted by *The Congregationalist*, a weekly church publication in Boston, for its Independence Day edition the following summer. Katharine wrote to the editor, politely requesting some changes to the words. They were printed for the first time on July 4, 1895, in the paper's "Home" column, and introduced with keen praise: "Miss Bates's poem has the true patriotic ring, pertinent to Fourth of July."

The new little verse was immediately noticed by a surprisingly large audience. And a responsive one.

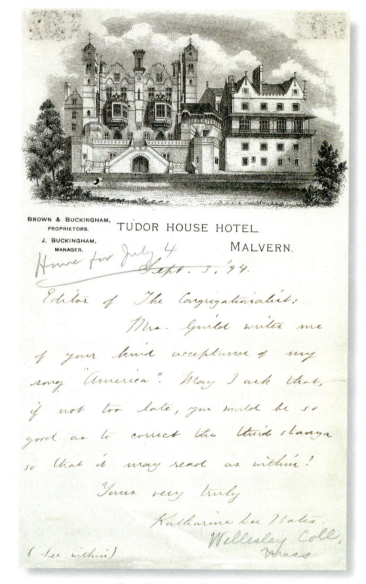

Her letter to the editor, 1894

AMERICA.

BY KATHARINE LEE BATES.

O beautiful for halcyon skies,
  For amber waves of grain,
For purple mountain majesties
  Above the enameled plain!
    America! America!
  God shed his grace on thee
Till souls wax fair as earth and air
  And music-hearted sea!

O beautiful for pilgrim feet,
  Whose stern, impassioned stress
A thoroughfare for freedom beat
  Across the wilderness!
    America! America!
  God shed his grace on thee
Till paths be wrought through wilds of thought
  By pilgrim foot and knee!

O beautiful for glory-tale
  Of liberating strife,
When once and twice, for man's avail,
  Men lavished precious life!
    America! America!
  God shed his grace on thee
Till selfish gain no longer stain
  The banner of the free!

O beautiful for patriot dream
  That sees beyond the years
Thine alabaster cities gleam
  Undimmed by human tears!
    America! America!
  God shed his grace on thee,
Till nobler men keep once again
  Thy whiter jubilee!

The Congregationalist, 1895, the poem's first time in print

The Congregationalist was a popular journal whose circulation reached far beyond New England and the church hierarchy. And while the poem contained some awkward terms that would not survive the decade ("halcyon" and "enameled" and the apocalyptic "whiter jubilee," among others), its simple beauty and raw emotion struck an immutable chord. Americans embraced her lines and started setting them to music—all kinds of music. First in print was a prominent composer named Silas G. Pratt, whose patriotic credentials had been certified when he directed three bands and more than 75,000 singers at the Fourth of July celebration during the Chicago World's Fair. Bates had missed the festivities by one day, and there is no evidence the two ever met. But Pratt wrote his tune the year the poem came out, and with permission from the author he published it in his book, *Famous Songs*. It was just the beginning of a symphony of "America the Beautiful" compositions over the next twenty years.

"No one was more amazed than I at the way the hymn was taken up," Katharine Lee Bates later recalled, telling one admiring audience, "When I found that you really wanted to sing it, I rewrote it in some respects to make it a bit more musical." The skies became "spacious," the plains "fruited," the third verse underwent some streamlining, and the "whiter jubilee" was judiciously replaced by a repeat of the glorious first refrain. On November 19, 1904, it was published as revised in the *Boston Evening Transcript*, the largest and most influential daily in New England. The single-column editorial heralded the poem as our new "national hymn...a thoroughly American production well-nigh perfect as poetry."

Once again Americans read the poem and spontaneously broke out in song. In Rochester, New York, a clergyman named Clarence A. Barbour from Lake Avenue Baptist Church came across the words in the *Transcript* and immediately felt "they should be used as a hymn…. They seemed to me to have a beauty and a message which would make them particularly useful." So Dr. Barbour and his wife, an accomplished musician, turned to the hymnal and looked through the metrical index to find a melody that matched the rhythm of the poem. "After trying a number of other tunes, we came to 'Materna,'" he later wrote to a friend, "and I at once felt that this was the tune to which the words could be most wisely joined."

A word here about hymnals. The practice of applying an available tune to a new text is ancient, deriving from the days when psalms were printed without music. But the meter, or the number of syllables in each line, was always included ("Amazing Grace," for instance, is 8, 6, 8, 6, known as Common Meter), so the faithful could put the words to a tune they already knew. The metrical index simplified the job.

By the time Dr. Barbour saw the *Boston Evening Transcript* in 1904, Sam Ward's "Materna" had been printed in a number of hymnals for more than a decade. It was listed in the index with "O Mother Dear Jerusalem" as Common Meter Double, or CMD (8, 6, 8, 6, 8, 6, 8, 6). That is precisely the cadence of the lines of Katharine Lee Bates' poem.

And that is how it came to the attention of ministers like Dr. Barbour. Although his claim to have made the connection before anyone else is not confirmed, it is

BOSTON EVENING TRANSCRIPT.

THE LISTENER

We rather guess that Professor Katherine Lee Bates of Wellesley has written the American national hymn; that is to say, if now it can be wedded to music of its own quality. Smith's "America" is fixed beyond recovery in an English tune, and the British national hymn at that. Keller's American hymn has now one set of verses and now another, the best of all being, of course, Dr. O. W. Holmes's "Angel of Peace," written for the Peace Jubilee. Julius Eichberg's "American Hymn" was given words smacking of a German adaptation. Now here is a thoroughly American production well-nigh perfect as poetry, and in the most exalted strain as politics. America has only to live up to the aspirations here breathed to realize its Golden Age,—the Golden Age of those idealists of late held in scant respect, the Fathers of the Declaration and the Constitution. As for what may be considered the physiography of the poem, Smith's Miltonic picture in those supposedly matchless lines

"I love thy rocks and rills
Thy woods and templed hills"

is fairly mated by Miss Bates's:

"O beautiful for spacious skies,
For amber waves of grain,
For purple mountain majesties
Above the fruitful plain!"

Then the course of national history is "touched in," as artists say, with not less of comprehensive and literal truth than of fine poetic imagery, in the next verse:

O beautiful for pilgrim feet,
Whose stern, impassioned stress
A thoroughfare for freedom beat
Across the wilderness!
America! America!
God mend thine every flaw,
Confirm thy soul in self-control,
Thy liberty in law!

And now comes the most beautiful and exalted of all the hymn's nobility of thought, uttering the patriot's prayer and faith in America's perfectibility:

O beautiful for glory-tale
Of liberating strife,
When valiantly, for man's avail,
Men lavished precious life!
America! America!
May God thy gold refine
Till all success be nobleness,
And every gain divine!

O beautiful for patriot dream
That sees beyond the years
Thine alabaster cities gleam
Undimmed by human tears!
America! America!
God shed his grace on thee,
And crown thy good with brotherhood
From sea to shining sea!

Have we an American composer to fit this noble poem to music "not too good for human nature's daily food," and so make the whole the "one entire and perfect chrysolite" of a national hymn?

∴ + +

The Boston Evening Transcript, 1904,
the poem's second version

entirely possible that the Lake Avenue congregation was the first in the nation to sing the Bates poem with the Ward tune, in November 1904. The new song was such a hit that a local grammar school principal included it in commencement exercises the following week. As it became a staple in the Rochester repertoire, word spread to other communities. Simultaneously, choirs and choruses across the country found "Materna" on their own, putting the new song on the lips of even more Americans.

In 1910, after Dr. Barbour had left his pastorate to work with the YMCA, he edited a book called *Fellowship Hymns*. The first one chosen, he later said, was the one that became No. 266. It was the first time Katharine Lee Bates's words appeared in print with Samuel Augustus Ward's music, making it available to an even wider audience. Two years later it appeared in a songbook for the Massachusetts Agricultural College in Amherst (now the University of Massachusetts at Amherst) and in a collection by a New Jersey man. He included "America the Beautiful" with "Materna" "partly because '*America! America!*' rings out so well in it."

Sad to say, the composer never knew the impact of his towering creation. Sam Ward died on September 28, 1903, from erysipelas, an infectious skin disease. The obituary in the Newark *Daily Advertiser* called him "one of the best known musical men in the State" and somberly assured its readers, "Everything was done to save Mr. Ward's life. Dr. H.C.H. Herold attended him and he had a trained nurse. He sank rapidly yesterday and last night hope was given

up. He was unconscious at the end. His wife and daughter were at his bedside." There was no mention of "Materna."

Samuel Augustus Ward

The Kingdom—National

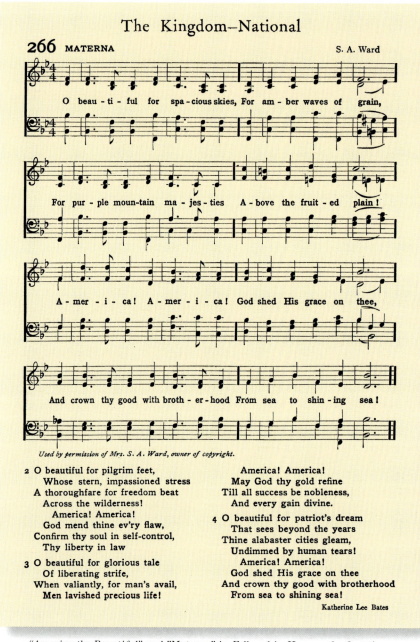

266 MATERNA   S. A. Ward

O beau-ti-ful for spa-cious skies, For am-ber waves of grain,

For pur-ple moun-tain ma-jes-ties A-bove the fruit-ed plain!

A-mer-i-ca! A-mer-i-ca! God shed His grace on thee,

And crown thy good with broth-er-hood From sea to shin-ing sea!

Used by permission of Mrs. S. A. Ward, owner of copyright.

2 O beautiful for pilgrim feet,
   Whose stern, impassioned stress
A thoroughfare for freedom beat
   Across the wilderness!
      America! America!
   God mend thine ev'ry flaw,
Confirm thy soul in self-control,
   Thy liberty in law

3 O beautiful for glorious tale
   Of liberating strife,
When valiantly, for man's avail,
   Men lavished precious life!

America! America!
   May God thy gold refine
Till all success be nobleness,
   And every gain divine.

4 O beautiful for patriot's dream
   That sees beyond the years
Thine alabaster cities gleam,
   Undimmed by human tears!
      America! America!
   God shed His grace on thee
And crown thy good with brotherhood
   From sea to shining sea!

Katherine Lee Bates

*"America the Beautiful" and "Materna" in Fellowship Hymns, the first time
the words and music were published together, 1910*

Meanwhile, Katharine Lee Bates was still polishing her little masterpiece. In 1911 she published the final version, the one we know today, giving it a proper name and star billing in her new book, *America the Beautiful and Other Poems*.

In an era of burgeoning nationalism, as the shadow of war darkened Europe and ultimately summoned our own soldiers, "America the Beautiful" was increasingly sung throughout the land, most often to the stately yet simple "Materna." But it was not the only melody, not by far.

Some put the words to the tune of "Auld Lang Syne"; some to an Irish classic called "The Harp that Once Through Tara's Halls." "It goes remarkably smooth to that air," a helpful correspondent informed Bates. And an astonishing number of people wrote their own music. An early composition came from Clarence C. Hamilton, a colleague in the Wellesley Music Department. It would be the students' choice for many years. Will C. MacFarlane, the municipal organist in Portland, Maine, where Katharine's brother Arthur lived, wrote a tune that repeated the "*America!*" refrain at the end of each stanza. It would be the implicit family favorite for decades.

The compositions came from close friends and total strangers, from men and women, blacks and whites, from every part of the country. A woman from Cambridge sent along music she had written because the poem "haunted" her. A voice teacher who tried his hand acknowledged that if she didn't like his music, "the wastebasket is handy." One day Katharine Lee Bates counted up seventy-four separate scores.

AMERICA THE BEAUTIFUL

O BEAUTIFUL for spacious skies,
    For amber waves of grain,
For purple mountain majesties
    Above the fruited plain!
      America! America!
God shed His grace on thee
And crown thy good with brotherhood
    From sea to shining sea!

O beautiful for pilgrim feet,
    Whose stern, impassioned stress
A thoroughfare for freedom beat
    Across the wilderness!
      America! America!
God mend thine every flaw,
Confirm thy soul in self-control,
    Thy liberty in law!

O beautiful for heroes proved
    In liberating strife,
Who more than self their country loved,
    And mercy more than life!
      America! America!
May God thy gold refine,
Till all success be nobleness,
    And every gain divine!

O beautiful for patriot dream
    That sees beyond the years
Thine alabaster cities gleam
    Undimmed by human tears!
      America! America!
God shed His grace on thee
And crown thy good with brotherhood
    From sea to shining sea!

"America the Beautiful," 1911, its final revision

I couldn't tell from just looking at the music how good—or bad—it was, so I asked for help from my friend Marvin Hamlisch, the multitalented virtuoso whose songs and performances have helped define America's modern musical taste. If I provided the scores would he play and rate them? He gave me a quick and generous "Yes," and a few weeks later I showed up at his piano bench with thirty-six sheets of music. By the end of the evening, I was exhausted and he was still good-naturedly analyzing the tunes.

To be sure, some of them were totally forgettable. "Too romantic, too genteel," he said of one. "It's a waltz, not a song about a country." Another was "too small, too tender. It sounds like a prayer." In several the tempo was too fast: "How can that possibly hit your heart? It's just for marines to march to." His comments were precise and often merciless:

"You know what this sounds like? A barbershop quartet."

"Dull verse."

"This one's an organ processional, what you play before the bride comes down the aisle."

"It's a tarantella, in 6/8 time. So Italian."

"Too sophisticated." (Here Hamlisch paused to let me in on a trick of the trade. "When I write, if I want people to hum the song," he said, "I keep that in mind. It can't be too difficult." Then he went on.)

"Too complicated."

"Lousy melody."

"Unmemorable."

"Oh God. Just purely bad."

But some held real promise, and I was riveted as the man who wrote "The Way We Were" and "They're Playing Our Song" sang and played his way through some very melodious versions of "America the Beautiful" that hadn't been heard for nearly a century. It was odd to pair the familiar words with such unknown music. But Hamlisch liked the way one composer set the "*purple mountain majesties*," a flowing melody whose notes ascended to go "*a-bove the fruited plain.*" "Listen to how good that is!" He admired an early score for a pleasant line but stopped midway through another on "*America!*" because the notes didn't go up, they went down. "Disappointing."

In the end, all the scores paled in comparison to "Materna," mostly because—both musically and there-fore emotionally—they didn't "get your heart." Sam Ward, Hamlisch pointed out, knew how to do that. And although the Bates words didn't exist when he wrote the music, he was clearly "a choirmaster who knew how to write for the voice." Hamlisch cited the subtle "repeti-tion of the rhythm: dotted quarter-eighth-quarter-quarter," as in "*BEAU-ti-ful for.*" He said the piece was "very American—very direct, straightforward." And he pointed out the musical secret in the refrain. At "*plain,*" the note we're on is tenuous and we feel unsettled, so the music takes us down to the keynote for the first syllable of "*America!*" That resolves the musical unease. Then Ward transports us on that great sweep up the scale so we can belt out the rest of the refrain. Or as Hamlisch put it, "he goes up and goes somewhere and gets your heart. No question, Sam Ward definitely did it best."

It is a sentence Katharine Lee Bates never uttered. Whenever anyone wrote to her to ask which version she liked best, the author refused to make a choice. Or to offer any criticism. She said the music just wasn't her responsibility. "I have always refrained from expressing a preference among the tunes," she once explained, "as it seems fit that the choice should be made by the singers rather than the writer."

She felt no such timidity about the words. Despite creative suggestions from scores of self-appointed critics, she insisted her version of the poem was the only one to sing. The recommendations redefined *chutzpah*. A gentleman from Ohio wrote a long, windy explanation of why she should change the word "stern" to "firm," and use "sages" rather than "patriot." He also advised that "'freedom' expresses the idea more satisfactorily than 'mercy' in the last line of the last stanza." A hymnbook editor from Rochester begged her to replace "alabaster" with "some word or phrase more clearly significant of American ideals." A fellow from New Hampshire stumbled over the same word: "What,' I say to myself, are alabaster cities?" People wanted her to remove the word "beautiful," to rhyme "proved" with something other than "loved." Bates rejected all the suggestions with a polite and firm (never stern) hand. And she gave the poem freely to all who would use it—on one condition: that users "scrupulously follow the authorized version." Why? "So that we may not have as many texts as we already have tunes," she said. And so there would be no more embarrassing little moments.

I can illustrate the need of this precaution from a single line
"O beautiful for patriot dream,"

which I have seen in more than one newspaper copy
"O beautiful for patriot drum,"
but which reached its climax of effect as printed in a church leaflet for a farewell meeting to the young soldiers of the town, boys self-conscious enough in their new khaki without the blushes induced by the chorused compliment,
"O beautiful for patriot dress."

Curiously, she did not protest when the poem was translated into other languages and applied to other countries. "I didn't have Australia in mind when I wrote it," she said agreeably, "but if they can use it and like it that is all right." There were also versions sung in Germany, the Philippines, India, Burma ("Beautiful Burma"), Canada, and Mexico, where the Spanish text was quite peppy:

Mi México! Mi México!
Bendigate el senor
su gracia de haasta rebosar
Del uno al otro mar

In this country the song was fast becoming an American tradition. No matter what the tune, it was played from Maine to California and sung from South Dakota to South Florida. It was printed in textbooks, poetry books, hymnals, and elementary school readers. During World War I, the troops who crossed the ocean to fight in the trenches of Europe carried not only their rifles but a pocket-sized publication from the U.S. government called *Songs of the Soldiers and Sailors*.

"America the Beautiful" was on page 15. A year later, the War Department's *Army Song Book* moved it up to page 12, lodging the song more securely in the hearts of more than one million doughboys. If George M. Cohan's "Over There" was the jaunty theme that took them to war, "America the Beautiful" was what they were fighting for. It was also the song they brought home.

Over time, Katharine Lee Bates received requests to use her words from anthologists, churches, Boy Scouts, the Colonial Dames of America, the National Council of Jewish Women, the Berkeley (Calif.) public schools, the State of Mississippi Forestry Commission, and the Victor Talking Machine Company of Camden, New Jersey, which wanted to include her poem in a brochure entitled "The Victrola in Americanization." She agreed to anything that was reasonable. She also fulfilled the seemingly endless requests for her wisdom, her autograph, even for multiple copies of the poem written out in her own hand. By the mid 1920s, she had adopted her family's irreverent nickname for the poem—"A. the B."—and devoted an entire cupboard in her house to the mounting correspondence. "I have been working like a beaver, day after day, going over the crowded contents of the A. the B. closet," she wrote her brother, almost overwhelmed by the flood of her success.

Keep in mind, she was running Wellesley's English department through all of this, and writing other poems, and publishing literary criticism. "America the Beautiful" was never the sole focus of her life, and she seemed content to let it seek its own level on the national hit parade. But finally she went along with an event that would seal its musical fate.

Although a Florida minister gushed to Bates that so many tunes meant "P O P U L A R I T E E E E E You are 'it,'" the multiplicity of melodies confused, frustrated, and dissatisfied others. As far back as 1904, the venerable Boston *Evening Transcript* had urged that the poem "be wedded to music of its own quality…. Have we an American composer to fit this noble poem to music?" And in 1918 Sylvester Baxter, a friend of Bates and a columnist for the Boston *Herald*, complained that the song, though "sung through the land," had "no distinctive music" yet identified with it. He wrote that "the sense of serene expanse conveyed by the words '*spacious skies*' calls for an evenness in the music and not the restlessness of a dotted quarter note that 'Materna' gave it."

The National Federation of Music Clubs (NFMC) took up the cause in 1926. Clearly miffed by the popular acceptance of a tune written for something else, they dismissed "Materna" as "an obvious anomaly that cries out for rectification" and held a nationwide contest for, as they bluntly put it, "a truly adequate setting" of the song. The stakes were high. A $500 prize and instant fame would go "to the American-born composer whose setting best expresses the love, loyalty and majesty its lines express." That despite the objections of a committee member that "the people have chosen and have chosen 'Materna,' and it will be worse than useless to try to force even a better tune upon them."

The three-month competition generated headlines around the country and an astounding 961 entries. Katharine Lee Bates made sure that existing melodies were also considered, but she otherwise maintained her

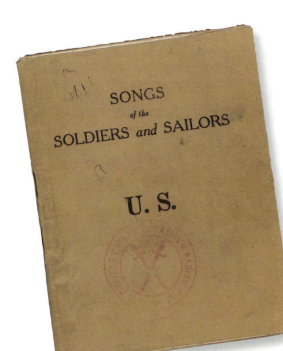

American troops in World War I took the new song overseas

A CALL TO THE AMERICAN COMPOSER

from the

Past Presidents Assembly

of

The National Federation of Music Clubs

President of the Federation
MRS. EDGAR STILLMAN KELLEY
Oxford, Ohio

National Chairman of the Assembly
MRS. WILLIAM ARMS FISHER
Boston, Mass.

By chance the inspired lines of Katharine Lee Bates' great patriotic hymn *America, the Beautiful* were printed a few years ago in a song book with the hymn-tune known as *Materna*. This tune was written by Samuel A. Ward forty years ago to match the plaintive seventeenth century hymn "O Mother dear, Jerusalem, when shall I come to Thee?" which it expresses admirably. But to forcibly combine music written to express the longing of a world-weary soul for a far-off heaven with Miss Bates' majestic lines glowing with a lofty patriotism is an obvious anomaly that cries out for rectification.

Over sixty attempts have been made to give *America, the Beautiful* a proper musical setting, and while several of them have had a limited circulation, none of them have sung their way into universal favor, or have the outstanding qualities that belong to a hymn for a great nation to sing "from sea to shining sea."

The Past Presidents Assembly of the National Federation of Music Clubs, with the permission and hearty approval of Katharine Lee Bates, now sponsors a nation-wide contest for a truly adequate setting of *America, the Beautiful*.*

A cash prize of $500 is to be awarded to the American-born composer whose setting best expresses the love, loyalty and majesty its lines express.

The prize setting will be presented to the Nation without copyright restriction so that it may be freely printed in every newspaper, magazine, hymn and song-book throughout the land and by every music publisher.

The wives of the Governors of all the States of the Union are to have the honor of contributing $1000 of the fund for the prize award and for the necessary expenses of carrying out this national contest. As *America, the Beautiful* was written by a woman of Massachusetts, and first appeared in print in Boston, July 4, 1895; and as the contest was proposed by the National Chairman of the Past Presidents Assembly, also a resident of Massachusetts; as the opening lines first

*The *Past Presidents Assembly* is an auxiliary group composed of those who have served as the president of a regularly organized music club, State Music Federation, or other music organization, or as District or National President of the National Federation of Music Clubs. It was founded at the Asheville Biennial on June 14, 1923, to weld into one compact, nation-wide fellowship all the past leaders in music clubdom in the United States.

floated into the author's mind on the summit of Pike's Peak, and the first four stanzas were penciled in her note book in Colorado; as the President of the National Federation of Music Clubs is a resident of Ohio; as the official action has just been taken at a meeting in Memphis, Tennessee; and as the National Federation of Music Clubs had its inception at the World's Fair in Chicago in 1893, and as the symbolic beauty of that White City quickened the poet's mind at the same time; the wives of the Governors of Massachusetts, Colorado, Ohio, Tennessee and Illinois head the honor subscription list.

The privilege of securing the funds in question is delegated to the State Chairmen of the Past Presidents Assembly and State Presidents of the National Federation of Music Clubs.

Conditions of the Contest

1. The contest is open to every native-born American musician regardless of his residence.
2. The setting of *America, the Beautiful* is to be for mixed voices in hymn-form and in vocal range and character fitted for mass singing.
3. The judges are to be men of national reputation and will be instructed to award the prize of $500.00 only to a truly noble setting of the text worthy of adoption as a hymn for the Nation.
4. The contest closes on Tuesday, March 1st, 1927.
5. Manuscripts are to be sent to the Chairman of the Contest, Mrs. William Arms Fisher, 362 Commonwealth Ave., Boston.
6. All manuscripts must be in ink, carry a *nom de plume* and be accompanied by a sealed envelope containing the full name and address of the composer with postage for its return.
7. Contestants are limited to a single unpublished setting, but at the request of Miss Bates, revisions by the composers of their published settings will be considered.
8. The prize setting is to be without any copyright restriction whatever and may be freely printed and freely performed.
9. The announcement and presentation of the award will be made in Chicago, Thursday evening, April 21st, 1927 at the banquet of the Past Presidents Assembly, when the hymn will first be sung. On the following evening it will be sung in Chicago by a thousand trained voices as the climax of the Singing Biennial of the National Federation of Music Clubs.

MRS. WILLIAM ARMS FISHER
National Chairman of the Past Presidents Assembly, and
First Vice-President of the National Federation of Music Clubs

Boston, Nov. 26, 1926

neutrality. Although contestants were directed to send new submissions to the Boston office, some made personal appeals to the author, unaware of her hands-off policy. The president of a music college in Seattle tried the hereditary approach:

> I am a descendant of two Colonial Governors of Massachusetts, Governors Dudley and Bradstreet, and of our first Poetess of New England, Anne Dudley Bradstreet. Our family numbers Oliver Wendell Holmes, William Ellery Channing,…Dr. Howe and Julia Ward Howe.
>
> I am from Essex Country, Mass., the home of Whittier, Lucy Larcom, Hawthorne, and many other celebrated Humans.

The manufacturer of shirts in Fall River, Massachusetts, mounted a more direct line of attack:

> I am enclosing manuscript of music which I have written for "America the Beautiful," and I trust you will find it brings out the sentiments expressed in your wonderful poem more effectively than the melodies written heretofore.

Bates left her assistant the usual instructions on this one: "Please return. I am, of course, declining to comment on his setting." She added that "the new settings are now coming in at the rate of three or four a day."

On the day of decision, tension was running high. Here is how the NFMC journal described the moments before the April 22, 1927, Midnight Frolic in the Gold Ballroom of Chicago's Congress Hotel:

> Everyone dressed in costumes—many of the most prominent men and women took part, even to dancing the minuet. There was great excitement in anticipation of hearing the new prize setting of "America the Beautiful." A hushed silence fell over the room.

And then, disappointment. The four nationally known music critics who served as judges announced that "although some of the settings showed fine musicianship, no one impressed us as reaching the high standard called for; none was fully adequate to the inspiring text." There would be no prize.

It was an unspoken and unconditional victory for the late composer, who didn't even know his music had been selected, let alone threatened. Or perhaps it was really a victory for the people. We sing "America the Beautiful" to "Materna" not by decree or law but simply because we like it.

Samuel Augustus Ward had understood the strength of his music. Katharine Lee Bates knew the value of fine words. "If I could write a poem people would remember after I'm dead," she once told a high school friend, "I would consider my life had been worth living." What neither had anticipated was the heartstopping effect of putting the two together.

THE MEANING

Sure, you know what it means. That's why the song is such a favorite. But this one gets even better when you look more closely.

"I can't read the lines through without swallowing hard," wrote a Massachusetts woman to the author, one in a stream of ecstatic letters. A New York City school superintendent confessed to Katharine Lee Bates that after hearing 628 students sing "America the Beautiful" at a graduation exercise, he wept. "I am not given to the shedding of tears, but the thrill of the sentiments of this composition on that occasion produced that effect on me…. That is a hymn which stirs a great emotion. It is an ode which voices high aspiration. I thank you and congratulate you."

"Look! Look, gentlemen! ... Purple mountains! Spacious skies! Fruited plains! ... Is someone writing this down?"

And then there was this one:

October 17, 1922
My Dear Miss Bates,
In this city of New Haven there is a Temporary
Home for children where we have about two
hundred and fifty children,—waifs who are
wards of the state and waiting for some kind
people to offer their home and foster parent-
age. Each day they open their singing time
with "America the Beautiful" and last Friday
I heard them bursting their throats with their
love for country and their joy in your hymn.
I suppose you have heard it sung thousands of
times, but you would have still another vision
of America could you hear the interpretation
given by these children, who have so little
to be thankful for…. Even the smallest shaver
there—a chubby cross-eyed Italian, with a
lusty soprano, tho only five,—could sing two
whole verses.
Joyfully yours,
Emily Sophie Brown

The song became a classic, sung at everything from presidential inaugurals to Girl Scout meetings, a universal expression of hope and patriotism. Even for non-Americans. When Pope John Paul II arrived in Boston for his triumphant visit in 1979—the first U.S. papal tour in history—he kissed the ground and then told the public, "I greet you America the Beautiful….

Permit me to express my sentiments in the lyrics of your own song: 'America, America, God shed His grace on thee.'"

The words alone were both celebration and prayer, repeatedly invoked in times of despair. In his speech to the nation before a joint session of Congress five days after the assassination of President John F. Kennedy, Lyndon B. Johnson, the new president, closed his remarks by asking the nation to "unite in these familiar and cherished words:

America, America,
God shed His grace on thee,
And crown thy good with brotherhood
From sea to shining sea."

Al Gore's concession speech after the bitterly divisive postelection turmoil of the 2000 presidential election summoned the same cooperation:

In the words of our great hymn, "America, America": "Let us crown thy good with brotherhood, from sea to shining sea."

What makes those words so meaningful? Why are they the ones we reach for to soothe and to celebrate?

Start with the fact that the woman who wrote them was deeply, intrinsically, probably genetically, a poet. "Hers was indeed a singing soul," said one of Katharine Lee Bates's Wellesley colleagues after her death. "I can hardly imagine what it must be like to have one's inner consciousness constantly ripple as hers must have done, in melody." A college classmate called her a "creative artist: seeing life in pictures, hearing it in great natural rhythms or intoxicating lilts; feeling it with a zest or a poignancy far beyond the general." To Katharine Lee Bates, the American coast from the deck of a steamer was "a line of lilac on the sea"; a wild storm was "a maddened blast"; she saw the moors of the British Isles as "one purple flush of heather, and the sky almost touching earth." Poetry came so naturally that she wrote nonsense verse for entertainment. And she was a relentless idealist, citing Charles Lindbergh's exhilarating flight across the Atlantic as proof

> that what the will of man
> Longs to do, it can.

Katharine's heart was also brimming with patriotism. The critic for *The Nation* read *America the Beautiful and Other Poems*, and pronounced the author "A lover of national themes who has learned to treat them sanely." Bates's sensible passion for her native land animates her earliest poems. America's gifts, she once observed, were the "least of her wealth"; this nation was clearly

> Something more
> Than cloud-enfolded hills or foam-lit shore,
> Or steepled towns.

Her ability to distill that "something more" from the century that shaped her is what gave us "America the Beautiful."

The America that Katharine Lee Bates inhabited and chronicled in 1893 was an energetic, optimistic and anxious country, throbbing with conflicting forces. No longer the rural, agricultural union she had been born into before the Civil War, it was an increasingly urban society. The population of 31 million in 1860 had more than doubled by the time she climbed Pikes Peak, swollen largely by the surge of new immigrants from Europe. And there were forty-four states, not thirty-three, all propelled toward the new century by a tide of unimagined inventions and discoveries: the telephone, the light bulb, the phonograph, the gas-engine automobile. In 1869 the transcontinental railroad reduced the vast land mass to a series of train rides. By the turn of the century, the heroes of America were the giants who had orchestrated its progress: John D. Rockefeller's Standard Oil Company was the largest oil trust in the world, Andrew Carnegie's Pittsburgh steel mills dominated global markets, and the fortunes controlled by financier J. P. Morgan effectively made him the central banker for the United States.

America was also undergoing a cultural explosion. Katharine was ten years old when *Little Women* appeared, a freshman in college when Mark Twain wrote *Tom Sawyer*. Her generation would witness the births of *Life* magazine and the *Ladies Home Journal*, the opening of Woolworth's first Five and Dime, and the invention of the game of basketball. The nation was not just changed, it was transformed.

But the widespread industrialization that pushed the country from farms to factories, from small family businesses to colossal corporations, from producers to consumers, created perplexing new problems. The enormous wealth of the few was offset by the dreadful poverty of many more. To some, the titans of American development were really robber barons exploiting the system and its people. Disabling strikes by disgruntled laborers plagued the workplace; political corruption thrived in the cities. At times, the center could not hold. The financial panic of 1893 sent more than 15,000 American businesses into receivership, closed more than six hundred banks, and put some 2.5 million people out of work. It was the worst economic depression the world had ever known.

The last decade of the century also marked a geographic milestone. In 1890, the Census Bureau announced that the American frontier no longer existed, because there were so many settlements in formerly isolated areas. That became the centerpiece of historian Frederick Jackson Turner's new theory. In a paper delivered at the Chicago World's Fair, just two weeks after Katharine Lee Bates left for Colorado, Turner said the Western frontier, not our European roots, defined the American character—our rugged individualism, our self-reliance, our democratic institutions. Its closing, he said, ended the first chapter of American history. By implication, it also threatened the very core of the nation: Would Americans still be Americans without wilderness to conquer?

Turner's theory has since been downplayed, especially since plenty of land remained to be homesteaded. But on the brink of the twentieth century, at the end of the so-called Indian Wars (Geronimo surrendered in 1886; Sitting Bull was killed in 1890, just before the

massacre at Wounded Knee), the idea of a gate slamming shut on the American adventure stoked the fin-de-siècle unease. The president of the Chicago World's Fair Commission put it another way: "We have no more continents to discover." Rapid growth had brought both confidence and uncertainty. The nation was on the verge of…something. But what? The fair itself offered one answer—a comforting vision of ordered architecture and industrial progress in a time of turbulence. Katharine Lee Bates gave us another.

The main themes of "America the Beautiful" are the ones Bates explored all her life: the wonder of nature, the vitality of our nation, its treasured past and infinite potential for the future. In her insightful biography, *Dream and Deed*, Bates's niece Dorothy Burgess explained her aunt's idealism in the poet's own words: "The heart must 'out-soar the hand.'" That notion is reinforced in the format of each verse: an opening celebration, a brief prayer, then a challenge to make something better. "America the Beautiful" is a portrait of America not only as it is, but as it could be.

O beautiful for spacious skies,
For amber waves of grain,
For purple mountain majesties
Above the fruited plain!

The poem begins with Bates's lifelong gratitude for the gifts of nature, deftly framing the spectacular images from her Western trip within her New England consciousness. Who but a child of the seacoast would

America the Beautiful, Then and Now

As Katharine Lee Bates first published it in The Congregationalist, 1895

O beautiful for halcyon skies,
For amber waves of grain,
For purple mountain majesties
Above the enameled plain!
America! America!
God shed his grace on thee
Till souls wax fair as earth and air
And music-hearted sea!

O beautiful for pilgrim feet,
Whose stern, impassioned stress
A thoroughfare for freedom beat
Across the wilderness!
America! America!
God shed his grace on thee
Till paths be wrought through
wilds of thought
By pilgrim foot and knee!

O beautiful for glory-tale
Of liberating strife,
When once and twice, for man's avail,
Men lavished precious life!
America! America!
God shed his grace on thee
Till selfish gain no longer stain
The banner of the free!

O beautiful for patriot dream
That sees beyond the years
Thine alabaster cities gleam
Undimmed by human tears!
America! America!
God shed his grace on thee,
Till nobler men keep once again
Thy whiter jubilee!

After Katharine Lee Bates revised it in 1904

O beautiful for spacious skies,
For amber waves of grain,
For purple mountain majesties
Above the fruited plain!
America! America!
God shed his grace on thee
And crown thy good with brotherhood
From sea to shining sea!

O beautiful for pilgrim feet,
Whose stern, impassioned stress
A thoroughfare for freedom beat
Across the wilderness!
America! America!
God mend thine every flaw,
Confirm thy soul in self-control,
Thy liberty in law!

O beautiful for glory-tale
Of liberating strife,
When valiantly, for man's avail,
Men lavished precious life!
America! America!
May God thy gold refine
Till all success be nobleness
And every gain divine!

O beautiful for patriot dream
That sees beyond the years
Thine alabaster cities gleam
Undimmed by human tears!
America! America!
God shed his grace on thee
And crown thy good with brotherhood
From sea to shining sea!

As Katharine Lee Bates revised it for the final time and published it in 1911. This is how we sing it today.

O beautiful for spacious skies,
For amber waves of grain,
For purple mountain majesties
Above the fruited plain!
America! America!
God shed His grace on thee
And crown thy good with brotherhood
From sea to shining sea!

O beautiful for pilgrim feet,
Whose stern, impassioned stress
A thoroughfare for freedom beat
Across the wilderness!
America! America!
God mend thine every flaw,
Confirm thy soul in self-control,
Thy liberty in law!

O beautiful for heroes proved
In liberating strife,
Who more than self their country loved,
And mercy more than life!
America! America!
May God thy gold refine
Till all success be nobleness
And every gain divine!

O beautiful for patriot dream
That sees beyond the years
Thine alabaster cities gleam
Undimmed by human tears!
America! America!
God shed His grace on thee
And crown thy good with brotherhood
From sea to shining sea!

see Kansas wheat growing in "waves"? And later define the scope of the continent by its waters? The obvious phrase is "ocean to ocean," which Bates had used in an earlier, less successful poem; "shining sea" is not only more lyrical, it's luminous.

> America! America!
> God shed His grace on thee
> And crown thy good with brotherhood
> From sea to shining sea!

This is the prayer, offered by a woman who belonged to no church and early rebelled against religious dogma. As a young teacher on the brink of promotion, Katharine Lee Bates nearly quit her job when Wellesley, in a glut of evangelical fanaticism, insisted that faculty members sign a pledge confirming their Christian beliefs. It was, Bates said, "intolerable" (a colleague called it "pietistic narrowness") that they question her "theological fitness," and she refused to reassure the English department of her "hold on 'the eternal verities'…I feel that I should be making the most sacred things of life sordid." The trustees wisely withdrew their demand, and Bates got her professorship. Her faith remained private and deep. But she was entirely comfortable in "America the Beautiful" invoking God's grace—as long as it was clear that it was an ecumenical appeal, all-inclusive, as spacious as the skies above. That's clear from the challenge that comes next—that the "good," or the natural bounty of the land, be enhanced with a spirit of community, of mutual respect. The word she uses is "brotherhood."

It's a good word, and the idea of living and working together as equals is one Katharine Lee Bates both advocated and practiced. She saw it firsthand in Falmouth, a whaling village where death at sea produced so many widows and orphans that the bonds of support sustained generation after generation. One of her students recalled her "passion for justice…her hope that sometime a star might be devised where living creatures need not prey on one another." That's the "brotherhood" of her poem. But it was written in the nineteenth century, long before words became weapons in the gender wars. Which is why recent generations of Wellesley students have changed it to "sisterhood." I cannot speak here for every alumna, but I personally want to assure you that our playful little conceit carries no disrespect and is rooted soundly in fact. Katharine Lee Bates fully understood the value of women's minds and lives.

In her preface to an edition of Tennyson's *The Princess*, a stinging satire of a woman's university, she protested the bias of an "exclusively masculine point of view," a position she'd resisted since childhood. In her childhood diary she rejoiced that women "have become impatient under the restraint men put upon them." She also decided, "I like women better than men." And signaling a lifelong resignation to her own genetic girth, "I like fat women better than lean ones." As an adult, successfully navigating a world run by men, Katharine Lee Bates headed a household of women. Her mother, her sister, Katharine Coman, and a steady stream of graduate students lived and worked in her brown-shingled house on Curve Street. As a teacher, she helped educate two generations of young women to make a difference in the world.

> O beautiful for pilgrim feet,
> Whose stern, impassioned stress
> A thoroughfare for freedom beat
> Across the wilderness!

The second verse celebrates our country's founders, who were "beautiful" because they crossed the continent (far less comfortably than she had) to spread our democracy. As for the "wilderness," the place Frederick Jackson Turner said no longer existed, Katharine Lee Bates knew that it was not virgin territory. Although she does not mention Native Americans in this poem, she was well aware of their civilization and their near annihilation, and elsewhere called the "shame of the Indian," like the "shame of the slave," one of the "blots" staining the country's past. This is presumably one of the shortcomings, or flaws, for which she now asks help, both divine and human.

> America! America!
> God mend thine every flaw,
> Confirm thy soul in self-control,
> Thy liberty in law!

America is not perfect, she is saying—a radical notion for a patriot—and we must tame our free spirit with "self-control," ground our prized freedom in the reason of law. Such discipline came naturally to this native New Englander, whose ethic included a lifetime devotion to work.

> O beautiful for heroes proved
> In liberating strife,
> Who more than self their country loved,
> And mercy more than life!

Despite her childhood horror after Abraham Lincoln's assassination and her pacifist leanings after World War I, Katharine Lee Bates had boundless praise for the courageous soldiers who fought the wars ("liberating strife") that produced a nation. The original text of this verse explicitly recalled both the Revolution and the Civil War ("when once and twice, for man's avail / men lavished precious life"), but the final version merges them into a single generic event, deflecting our attention from bloody battles to dedicated human beings. By putting the "heroes" first (and dropping the earlier reference to a "glory tale"), she also manages to honor the warriors without glorifying war. And their sacrifice encompasses everyone. In a later poem about Memorial Day services she would write that after the death of soldiers

> A woman's heart lies cold…
> Not to the men alone this rite belongs…
> There is no sex in courage and in pain.

In other words, you don't have to fight a war to be a hero.

This stanza is aimed at the greed of those Bates also called the "money-maddened throng." Like many disillusioned with the excesses of the Gilded Age, Katharine Lee Bates wanted to purify America's great wealth, to channel what she had originally called "selfish gain" into more noble causes. She didn't oppose material success—indeed she was awed by the century's great industrial progress—and this may be the only national song to put profit right up there with patriotism. But her dream demands more, asking that our successes—individual and national—reach beyond our own personal agendas, so they "no longer stain," as she'd first written, the grandeur of American freedom. She doesn't mention any corporate or political leaders by name, but the people who read and sang her words a century ago likely had their own candidates.

Finally, Bates talks about the future. Those "alabaster cities" that have baffled so many are not, as has been charged by some, a racist notion of all-white urban centers. Rather, they represent the dreamy vision of harmony and beauty that she saw on her trip to Chicago. This is Bates's translation of the White City of the World's Fair, the peaceful ideal that she hoped would appear on the other side of the century. Or centuries. In Chicago the buildings of the White City were an illusion—glowing facades on exhibition halls. Katharine Lee Bates recognized the ambition behind the effect as our hope for the future. But she was not seeing it with blinders.

Bates knew the other side of the American city—the poverty, the tenements, the hopelessness. Although her friend Katharine Coman lived in placid Oak Park (once described as the place where "the saloons stop and the church steeples begin"), she recognized the turmoil of those served at Hull House and had written a children's book exposing the "wretched, troublous life" of the sweatshops, its women bending over sewing machines in dreary closets with their "reeking walls" and "poisonous stench." She no doubt knew of the racism at the World's Fair—how blacks were kept out of power and out of the mainstream. Overseas, Bates was troubled by the inequities of class she observed in England and Spain. And while always more conservative than her reformist colleagues—she was a poet, not a politician—Katharine Lee Bates stood up for her share of social causes. She opposed capital punishment ("If Society was wise and strong and good, it would be able to convert its criminals into men instead of into corpses") and stopped wearing fur coats when she learned about the cruelty of steel traps, then lobbied against their use. She was a proud member of the faculty at the college Calvin Coolidge once called a political "hotbed of radicalism."

American patriotism on the eve of the first World War

So she knew that the sunny symbolism of the 1893 World's Fair was a goal, not yet a reality. "I saw America in the making," she later wrote of her stop in Chicago. It was there she realized "that against the smoke-stained, sin-stained city of the day there lay the possibility of some spiritual invention that should give us cities that were all beautiful." In "America the Beautiful" she is not suggesting that "human tears" aren't shed in our cities, or in our society, but that the awful problems we face today should not derail our dreams for the future. What's "undimmed" in her vision is the dream, not the cities. It is a powerful ideal of a country with a mission to carry out the promise of its founders. And it infuses her poem with a buoyant patriotism. We sing about our land and its people, not about a flag; about dreams of peace and equality, not the triumph of conquest. And when we reach the final refrain and repeat the prayer for unity and togetherness, it's, well…here's Marvin Hamlisch again, still animated.

"She has explained all the things that have gotten her to this point," he reminded me. "Look at the spacious sky, the amber waves, the mountains, the plains. What she gushes out is '*America! America!*' What both the melody and the lyric have in common is both gush, both explode at the same time. They both say, I can't hold in my emotions any longer. I've seen all this, it's so spectacular, and Wow! And the Wow! is '*America! America!*'"

Nearly a century earlier, a poet from Boston took it a step further. "It seems to me really the best of all our national anthems," he wrote in 1918. "I wish it might replace the 'Star-Spangled Banner.'" He wasn't the only one.

GREETINGS OF 4TH JULY

THE ANTHEM

If you come from Baltimore, you might want to skip this chapter. Or at least keep an open mind.

It's become as much of a cliff-hanger as the main event: the pregame tension over whether the celebrity singing "The Star-Spangled Banner" will actually make it to "the land of the free" or skid off-course on a sour note. One opera star admitted preparing for such appearances the same way the ballplayers themselves got ready: "I warm up long in advance and do a lot of worrying and pacing back and forth."

How did this strain on our vocal chords become our official music? Why this "heaven-piercing abomination" (and that's one of the milder assessments) rather than something we like to sing?

The American hunger for a national anthem dates back to the Civil War. It was May 1861, one month after Confederate guns shelled Fort Sumter. "The whole country quivered with a new emotion," wrote the distinguished essayist Richard Grant White. Union loyalists ached for a way to express their "patriotic feeling in verse." There were plenty of likely contenders, but none had sufficiently stirred the national soul. The "Star-Spangled Banner," born out of an American victory in the War of 1812, was curtly dismissed by White and others as "useless" and "unfitted" for the current conflict. So a contest was held for a new one.

As one of thirteen prominent citizens named to the selection committee, White was openly doubtful of the project, reluctant to assume a role better left to time and custom. He apologized for their audacity, admitting that "under ordinary circumstances, such a call would

CHARLESTON
MERCURY
EXTRA:

Passed unanimously at 1.15 o'clock, P. M., December 20th, 1860.

AN ORDINANCE

To dissolve the Union between the State of South Carolina and other States united with her under the compact entitled "The Constitution of the United States of America."

We, the People of the State of South Carolina, in Convention assembled, do declare and ordain, and it is hereby declared and ordained,

That the Ordinance adopted by us in Convention, on the twenty-third day of May, in the year of our Lord one thousand seven hundred and eighty-eight, whereby the Constitution of the United States of America was ratified, and also, all Acts and parts of Acts of the General Assembly of this State, ratifying amendments of the said Constitution, are hereby repealed; and that the union now subsisting between South Carolina and other States, under the name of "The United States of America," is hereby dissolved.

THE
UNION
IS
DISSOLVED!

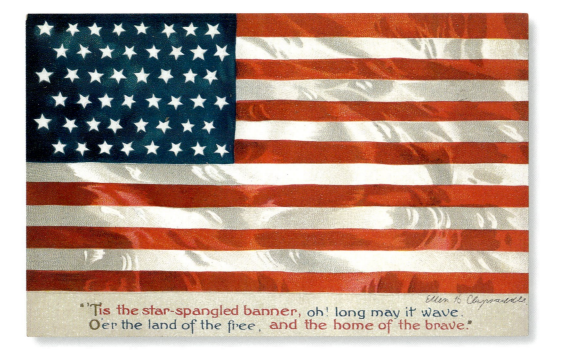

"'Tis the star-spangled banner, oh! long may it wave.
O'er the land of the free, and the home of the brave.'"

Ellen H. Clapsaddle

be almost ridiculous; for national hymns are born of occasion, not made to order. But the circumstances of the present time are very extraordinary." And so public entries were solicited. The goal was eloquently stated by one judge:

> Any truly patriotic national hymn is, of necessity, the great peace song and the great war song of the nation. It fits every emotion…. It is the national heart-beat set to music.

Richard Grant White was even more specific:

Let it be brimful of loyalty to the flag…. Let its allusions be to our fathers' struggle for national existence…let it have a strong, steady, rhythmical flow…. The music must…be…simple and strong, with a graceful, lively strength. A song which fulfilled these conditions…would pervade and penetrate, and cheer the land like sunlight.

O beautiful for spacious skies…
Unfortunately, little Katie Bates was still in diapers, so "America the Beautiful" wasn't available. But 1,200 compositions were submitted, some accompanied

Yankee Doodle

Father and I went down to camp, A-long with Captain Goodwin

And there we saw the men and boys As thick as hast-ty pud-ding

Yan-kee doo-dle keep it up.   Yan-kee doo-dle dan-dy,

Mind the mu-sic and the step, And with the girls be han-dy.

COPR. E.NASH 1909.

cannot invent a national song. "With comparatively few exceptions, the hymns sent in proved to be of interest only to their writers," reported the Civil War–era gentlemen. They were "commonplace," "unmitigated nonsense." For example:

> Our banner, our banner, long may it
> wave o'er us!
> And the bird of our freedom long fly
> on before us!

The most offensive entries were burned for fuel. The prize was withheld. There was no national song.

Which is not to say there was no music during the Civil War. Southerners marched to "Dixie" and "The Bonnie Blue Flag," while Northerners went into battle singing "Tramp, Tramp, Tramp (the Boys Are Marching)" and "John Brown's Body," among others. The tune of the latter rose to mythic status when poet Julia Ward Howe put new words to it after a moving visit with Union troops in 1861. Her poem was called "The Battle Hymn of the Republic," and its spiritual message came to symbolize the cause of the war itself.

But when the country was reunited, there was still no unifying music, no single song to make Americans feel American together. "Yankee Doodle," created during Revolutionary War days, was considered too childish, a comic burlesque. "Hail Columbia" seemed ordinary, unexceptional in words and music. The simply titled "America" ("My country 'tis of thee…"), written in 1832, remained a popular favorite for its unadorned tribute to country ("sweet land of liberty") and nature

by their own music, many more delivered with threats and bombastic utterances from authors desperate to win. By summer's end, the weary committee realize what the judges of the National Federation of Music Clubs would discover a century later when they sought a new melody for "America the Beautiful": You simply

("thy rocks and rills"). But the tune was England's— "God Save the Queen [or King]"—so the song rarely made it beyond the classroom.

The only one close to the people's choice—and it was far from a consensus—was "The Star-Spangled Banner." It was composed in 1814 by Francis Scott Key, a lawyer who witnessed the overnight British bombardment of Fort McHenry from a boat in the middle of Baltimore's harbor. When Key realized the American fort—and flag—were "still there" the next morning, he pulled out a letter from his pocket and wrote his poem on the back. Within months it was published, accompa-nied by an eighteenth-century melody that had been written for an English gentlemen's club. The tune, "To Anacreon in Heaven," was named for a Greek poet who celebrated wine and women in song, making it the sub-ject of much derision in later days. But at the time it was distributed so widely, people began to include it at patriotic events. By the turn of the century, U.S. Army and Navy bands played it at official ceremonies.

In 1912 the first of a continuum of bills to make "The Star-Spangled Banner" the national anthem was introduced in Congress, setting off a lively debate during the next two decades over its virtues and flaws. On the

ORIGINAL STAR SPANGLED BANNER, U. S. NATIONAL MUSEUM, SMITHSONIAN INSTITUTION   4A-H2188

THE STAR-SPANGLED BANNER

Oh, say, can you see, by the dawn's early light,

"LONG MAY IT WAVE."

And besides, one entire verse (the third) was full of hatred toward our staunchest allies, the British—who had been our enemy when Key wrote in his poem

> **Their blood has wash'd out their foul footsteps' pollution…**

Of course, most people didn't realize that because they didn't know the words, a fact that President Harding lamented publicly in 1923. He had been listening to people sing "The Star-Spangled Banner," and said "nearly all were mumbling their words, pretending to sing. Somehow I would like to see the spirit of American patriotism enabled to express itself in song."

But the biggest criticism was that the song was just too militaristic, too violent, too hostile for a nation committed to peace. Bill after bill died in committee without ever coming to a vote. During a 1923 debate on the floor of the House of Representatives, Rep. Ira Greenlief Hersey, Republican of Maine, confronted the sponsor of that year's attempt, New York Democrat Emanuel Celler:

one hand, it was a "quickening, constructive, powerful anthem that makes vibrant the forces American," said one supporter. On the other, the range—more than an octave and a half—was too broad. The event was too specific, the words taxed the memory. "They paint a picture, they do not embody a sentiment," Richard Grant White had said. It was of "local character and queer phraseology," sniffed a New Jersey woman in 1916.

Mr. Hersey: This is a military anthem, of course.
Mr. Celler: I should say it would be; yes.
Mr. Hersey: In the age in which we live, striving for peace with all nations and peoples and among ourselves, do you think it is exactly proper to adopt a national anthem which is a military anthem?
Mr. Celler: It is not military in that sense. It is not military in the sense that it arouses

military furies or military passions. Every national anthem is military in a way.

Mr. Hersey: You mean of other nations?

Mr. Celler: Yes.

Mr. Hersey: That is no reason why we should adopt a military anthem.

No one ever accused "America the Beautiful" of militarism, a primary factor in the growing effort to make *it* the national anthem.

"It is without the note of jingo patriotism which mars 'The Star-Spangled Banner,'" said one fan. "It has no suggestion of national brag or of regrettable history."

"It IS America; not a petty naval action in a half-forgotten petty war, fitted to the semi-unsingable air of a ponderous old English booze-song," wrote the novelist Albert Payson Terhune to his friend Katharine Lee Bates. "I am not the first nor the only writer who, in public print, has asked that 'America the Beautiful' be substituted for 'The Star-Spangled Banner' as our anthem.… I love every line of it…because it is poetry and noble; while Key's effusion is hysteric and false-quantified doggerel, at best." In 1908 a Chicago lawyer wrote to President Theodore Roosevelt, saying "a poem of such remarkable beauty and strength" as "America the Beautiful" should be considered for "adoption as the National Air."

The appeal of the song deepened with U.S. involvement in World War I. Molly Dewson, a Wellesley graduate who would become a prominent New Deal Democrat, wrote from her post with the American Red Cross Bureau of Refugees, in Paris, on December 3, 1917:

Dear Miss Bates,—

Ever since I came over here I have meant to write you to tell you of such a pleasant happening which I thought would interest you.

We had reached France after a very unusual trip compared with peace time trips. A boatload of two or three hundred persons with one idea—to help France—and a twinge of danger—the submarines—is enough to make any trip unusual. Our trunks were piled ten high in the middle of a little open steamer and we were clustered around and over them in every square foot of space. No one could budge and there we sat or stood from one to ten while we steamed up the river to the dock. By seven o'clock it was dark and we were cold and hungry. Nothing to see, nothing to eat, nothing to do and all talked out. So I said to Betty Scott "Let's sing and forget." And we did, and which do you suppose was the one that went best? Yes, yours! A man from Colorado dug in his bag and snapped his electric torch on a little copy of it so that they could sing every verse. Betty and the girl from Atlanta and the one from the Middle West knew it better than our other national anthems but they wanted it right. They sang it three times and it sounded very, very lovely to me on that top-heavy boat rushing along in the darkness with only the dim misty lights of the shore.

Another woman wrote that same year from Boston to tell Bates about the 1,600 boys and girls of East High who "love your 'America the Beautiful.' They always sing it better than anything else at assemblies, and when they finish their enthusiasm bursts into applause. They seem to appreciate the splendid words more than ever this fall—as they should."

But the story Katharine Lee Bates treasured most came directly from the front lines on the day the Germans surrendered. She heard it from the sister of a soldier who was there, on November 11, 1918, on a battlefield in the Verdun sector of France. At the eleventh hour on the eleventh day of the eleventh month, after bitter fighting and brutal death, the armistice took hold and the firing stopped.

> A bewildering silence fell. The soldiers… stood speechless, staring at one another, or dropped to the ground. Then they saw on a hillside a battalion in formation and heard them singing "America the Beautiful," and they all came to life again and sang it with tears on their faces.

This story made the tears come on my own.

In stateside ceremonies, the song was sung at countless Armistice Days, an unofficial anthem that expressed, in the words of one admirer, "what we were privileged to feel."

In 1926, the National Hymn Society urged Congress to adopt "America the Beautiful" as the national hymn. As one sympathizer put it, "It expresses the highest and deepest emotions of patriotism, not in any spirit of militant aggression and world-conquering imperialism, but with a profound gratitude and affection for the country, the government, and the traditions that have made us what we are." Katharine Lee Bates, while visibly moved by the sentiment, made it clear to Society members at a luncheon in Boston that she would not participate in the campaign, and she refused to promote her own song at the expense of any other. Mindful of the ongoing competition to find new music for her poem—a venture in which she also took no part—she wrote her brother after the meeting, "It seems better not to bring the matter of adoption before Congress till the tune is to some degree settled. Personally, I don't believe the time is ripe for any such effort, but I am keeping out of the two enterprises."

But the idea was catching on. "America the Beautiful" was going one-on-one against "The Star-Spangled Banner," not least because its comfortable nine-note range (compared to the "Banner's" twelve) could actually be sung. In 1930, as the debate in Congress heated up, education experts at Columbia University announced their opposition to "The Star-Spangled Banner," saying its martial tone required "a feeling of danger" to be properly sung. One professor said it inspired the narrow patriotism of warlike activity and that he preferred the broader ideals of "love of home, neighborliness, good citizenship, pride in worthy accomplishment, regard for those great builders who have made our country what it is and an eagerness to emulate them. These elements are found in Katharine Lee Bates' lovely song…. If we have an official national anthem, it should be one whose effect upon the mental and spiritual development of our millions of school children will be in keeping with real patriotism."

The controversy boiled over in the letters and editorial columns of the nation's newspapers. This sampling from the *New York Times* illustrates the arguments:

> **February 3, 1930:** But worse than the music are the words of Key's poem… today both the sentiment and the language are outmoded and seem rather silly…. If we are to have a national anthem adopted by act of Congress, the words of Katharine Lee Bates' "America the Beautiful" are far more like what we want and need.

> **February 5, 1930:** "The Star-Spangled Banner" is [too] local. Its inspiration was a single event in a war that had little of an epic character and has been a single paragraph in our later and greater history…. "America the Beautiful" is the hymn that best expresses our idealism and it does that with breadth and loveliness. A national hymn, however, needs ruggedness and virility rather than loveliness. It is, of course, a hymn of peace. It could not be sung while advancing to gouge out the enemies' eyes.

> **February 12, 1930:** "America the Beautiful" will not do on account of its title, for we must admit that there are other countries which are far more beautiful than ours, and even if there were not,

one would not wish to be too boastful in our national anthem.

> **March 9, 1930:** As John Philip Sousa has said, "Nations will seldom obtain good national anthems by offering prizes for them. The man and the occasion must meet."

Many touched on what Congress had discussed some years earlier. Why did we need any *official* national anthem at all, let alone "The Star-Spangled Banner"?

Rep. Hatton William Sumners (D-Tex.):
>…I have never been so sure and I am becoming less sure of the wisdom of undertaking to give direction to the drift of public opinion by legislation rather than have that drift come up naturally….

Mr. Celler:
>…I think we must be actuated by patriotic motives and try to instill in the hearts of the people some idea of not the necessity, but of the benefits to be accrued from the widespread use of this song.

Mr. Sumners:
>The idea of a governmental guardianship of the people everywhere and all the time may not be involved here, but it is a thing that disturbs me.

Mr. Celler:
>I must perforce differ with you on whether or not we are drifting into a paternalistic form of government or otherwise. I do not think we ought to enter into that debate here at this present time.

"THE STAR-SPANGLED BANNER" NOT FAVORED BY EVERYBODY

One Writer, in Fact, Deplores Official Action on National Anthem as Tending to Increase Disrespect for Law

To the Editor of The New York Times:

May not the 5,000,000 petitioners be after all an aggressive minority trying to make the rest of us accept "The Star-Spangled Banner" by the compulsion of law? The rest of us, 120,000,000 strong, have not let our peep.

In such a matter wh say so of the Fe be sought? dividual as

use this song as a national anthem, let them by all me___ do so; but why box it up and na_____ de cree? Nobody k ture may bring t al composit us dignity f deep xpressi er th n.

'Star-Spangled Banner' Opposed as Anthem; Music Supervisors Vote Protest to Congress

Special to The New York Times.

CHICAGO, March 29.—Contending that the sentiments expressed in "The Star-Spangled Banner" are not representative of a peace-loving nation, the Music Supervisors National Conference, in session today, adopted a resolution protesting passage of a bill by Congress to adopt it as the national anthem.

The supervisors further asserted that the song was the outgrowth of a single historical event and was too difficult a musical composition to be rendered properly by school children, informal gatherings and public meetings where the singing of the national anthem was appropriate.

"America, the Beautiful," the music of which was written by Samuel A. Ward and the words by Katherine Lee Bates, was favored to replace "The Star-Spangled Banner," Miss Mabelle Glenn of Kansas City,

retiring president, was instructed to forward a copy of the resolution to Congress, which will consider the national anthem bill on April 7.

The resolution declared that "approval of this bill would signify to our people and to the world at large a unique endorsement of this tion," and "the text of the song not fully reflect the spirit of committed to peace.

"The Music Supervisors Conference," the resoluti ed, "with a membership with the support of the music educators who sical activities of mu in our schools and itual values in while recognizing of "The Star vigorously of one of our our national

---

WANT PEACE IDEAL IN NATIONAL ANTHEM

Experts at Teachers College Find "Star-Spangled Banner" Too Martial for Daily Use.

AGREE ON SONG'S BEAUTY

But Say It Should Be Replaced by "America the Beautiful" When We Are Not Facing War.

Education experts at Teachers College, Columbia University, announced yesterday that they opposed official recognition of "The Star-Spangled Banner" as the national anthem. In its place they urged the use of "America the Beautiful," by Katherine Lee Bates, because of the peace-time serenity of its words and music.

Their objection to "The Star-Spangled Banner," they said, were not prompted by the fact that it was sung originally with different words, in English taverns by boisterous tradesmen. What they opposed was its martial flavor, holding that the stimulating effect of "bombs bursting in air" was appropriate only on warlike occasions and that the song should not be taught to the children of a nation at peace.

Peter W. Dykem, a professor of music education at Teachers College, admitted that it ranked with the "Marseillaise" among the great national anthems, but said it required "a feeling of danger" to be properly sung.

The argument over the anthem

Rep. Andrew Jackson Montague [D-Va.]:

    We are not drifting; we have arrived.

Mr. Celler: We have jogged along for a century and most people want this song. I am sure they do. I have letters here from all over the country, from all kinds of organizations.

Mr. Sumners: There is nothing to keep them from singing it….

Still, the pressure for an official anthem—specifically, "The Star-Spangled Banner"—intensified. Petitions trailing millions of signatures piled up at the Capitol. Two sopranos appeared at the House Judiciary Committee to perform the song and refute the notion that its notes were beyond a singer's range. On April 21, 1930, the House passed its bill; on March 4, 1931, the Senate agreed and President Herbert Hoover signed it into law, making "The Star-Spangled Banner" the national anthem. There was no provision that citizens know the words.

But that didn't stop the debate. As the years passed, many Americans treated "America the Beautiful" as if it were the national anthem, or at least the one that counted in times of crisis. On the evening of December 7, 1941, the day the Japanese bombed Pearl Harbor, President Franklin D. Roosevelt met at the White House until past midnight with Congressional leaders, grim-faced as they departed. In the crisp, bitter cold, beneath a moon wrapped in mist, a small crowd gathered beyond the iron fence and tried to sing "America the Beautiful." One reporter noted in sadness that their voices "quavered badly."

In 1985, Representative Andy Jacobs Jr., an Indiana Democrat and former Marine, took on the cause anew, introducing a bill in the United States Congress to replace "The Star-Spangled Banner" with "America the Beautiful." H.R. 1052 "was a friend's idea," he told me, "but I started thinking about it, and agreed. I got banged up in one war, and that's one reason I have a strong interest in peace." An acknowledged iconoclast, Jacobs allowed that "The Star-Spangled Banner" had the power to stir our emotions, and he suggested it be reserved for "football games and other paramilitary events." But after six consecutive tries to get the law changed—a bill a year until he retired—he said he wasn't sanguine about the possibilities. "People in Congress are afraid of their shadows," he said. "They don't want controversy."

They also don't want their districts marginalized. A member from Baltimore rose to speak against the Jacobs bill and cited a unanimous resolution from the Baltimore City Council noting, among other reasons, that "unlike 'America the Beautiful,' 'The Star-Spangled Banner' has a hometown." That, of course, is Baltimore. Maryland Governor Donald Schaefer particularly took offense because his football team, the Baltimore Colts, had recently moved to Indianapolis. He told Andy Jacobs, "First they steal our Colts; now they want to steal our anthem."

The same mindset thwarted Rep. Margaret Heckler's earlier bills to make "America the Beautiful" the nation's bicentennial hymn, whatever that would have meant. A Republican from the town of Wellesley, Heckler liked the song and valued the fact that its author had lived in her district. "I tried to round up as

99TH CONGRESS
1ST SESSION

H. R. 1052

To make "America, the Beautiful" the national anthem of the United States of America.

IN THE HOUSE OF REPRESENTATIVES

FEBRUARY 7, 1985

Mr. JACOBS introduced the following bill; which was referred to the Committee on Post Office and Civil Service

---

A BILL

To make "America, the Beautiful" the national anthem of the United States of America.

1   *Be it enacted by the Senate and House of Representa-*
2 *tives of the United States of America in Congress assembled,*
3 That the Act entitled "An Act To make The Star-Spangled
4 Banner the national anthem of the United States of Amer-
5 ica", approved March 3, 1931, (46 Stat. 1508; 36 U.S.C.
6 170) is amended to read as follows:
7 "That the composition known as 'America, the Beautiful',
8 which consists of the poem entitled 'America, the Beautiful'
9 written by Katherine Lee Bates and the music entitled 'Ma-

2

1 terna' composed by Samuel Ward, is designated the national
2 anthem of the United States of America.".
3   SEC. 2. The title of such Act is amended by striking out
4 "The Star-Spangled Banner" and inserting in lieu thereof
5 " 'America, the Beautiful' ".

○

The first bill introduced by Rep. Andy Jacobs Jr., 1985

many co-sponsors as I could find," she recently recalled, "but the merits of the song were lost in the whole bicentennial fervor. Everyone thought their own state song should be considered. So it dissolved into a tug-of-war between the states."

In her own day, Katharine Lee Bates tried to defuse the rivalry. A devoted patriot who sprung to her feet whenever "The Star-Spangled Banner" was played, she wrote a letter to a newspaper about the move to elevate "America the Beautiful."

> [A]s to making it the national anthem, I am personally more than content with the heart-warming reception the song…has already had… I am glad to have it go as far as popular goodwill carries it. As for "pushing" it or "urging" it or striving to have it "supplant" something else, nothing could be more at variance with my constant attitude toward it nor more averse to my temperament.

But that doesn't stop the rest of us from trying. In 1988, the legendary Ray Charles lent his name to yet another attempt. The singer himself made the point vividly when he asked, "Honestly, wouldn't you rather sing about the beauty of America?"

Hamilton School
Weehawken, New Jersey
October 31, 1928

My Dear Miss Bates
    I like the song you wrote. It has a nice tune. We sing it in assembly every morning… "America The Beautiful" is the song we sing most. I wish it was our national song.
        Your friend,
        Robert Curtey

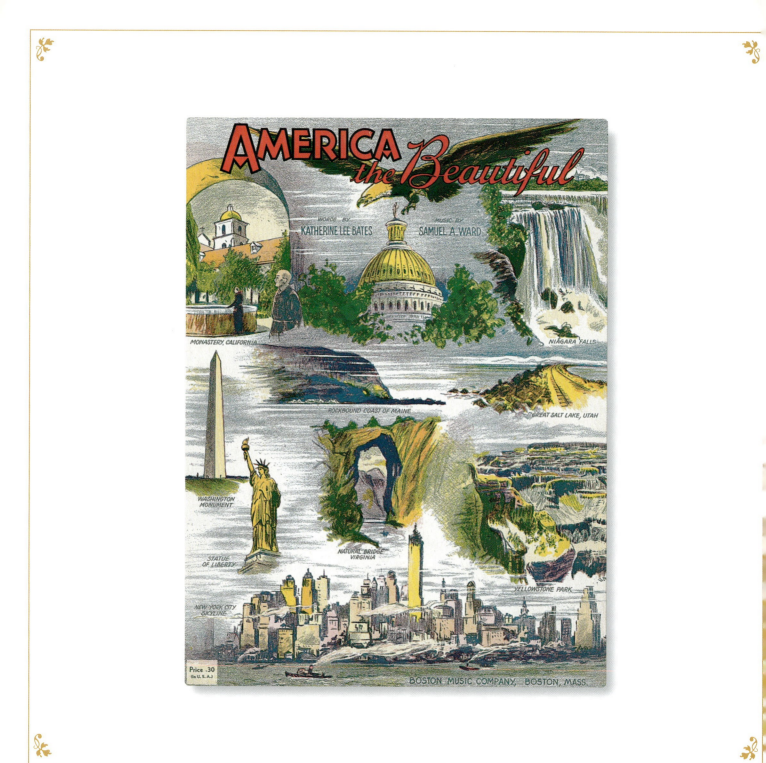

THE LEGACY

Toward the end of her life, after the song was embedded in the national psyche and the author had become a genuine celebrity, Katharine Lee Bates held fast to her belief that the enduring success of "America the Beautiful" was due to the public, not to herself. "That the hymn has gained, in these twenty-odd years, such a hold as it has upon our people," she once wrote, "is clearly due to the fact that Americans are at heart idealists, with a fundamental faith in human brotherhood."

Ray Charles first recorded "America the Beautiful" in 1972, a year when idealism and brotherhood were splintered by violent political dissent. He said his performance came straight from the heart, with no irony intended. "I'm the first to say this country is racist to the bone," he told author David Ritz. "But that doesn't mean I can't be patriotic. For all the bullshit about America, I still work and live here in comfort."

His captivating interpretation, by any measure the definitive version of the song, is more blues than anthem, a mellow riff with deep personal meaning. "Some of the verses were just too white for me," he explained. "So I cut them out and sang the verses about the beauty of the country and the bravery of the soldiers. Then I put a little country church backbeat on it and turned it my way." One critic wrote that he transformed the song into "a gospel anthem, stretching the words into shapes both painful and exultant." Charles was asked if adding the song to his repertory was his own idea. "Yes, darling, who else's idea would it be?"

Yes indeed.

Three years later, Elvis Presley got the same idea

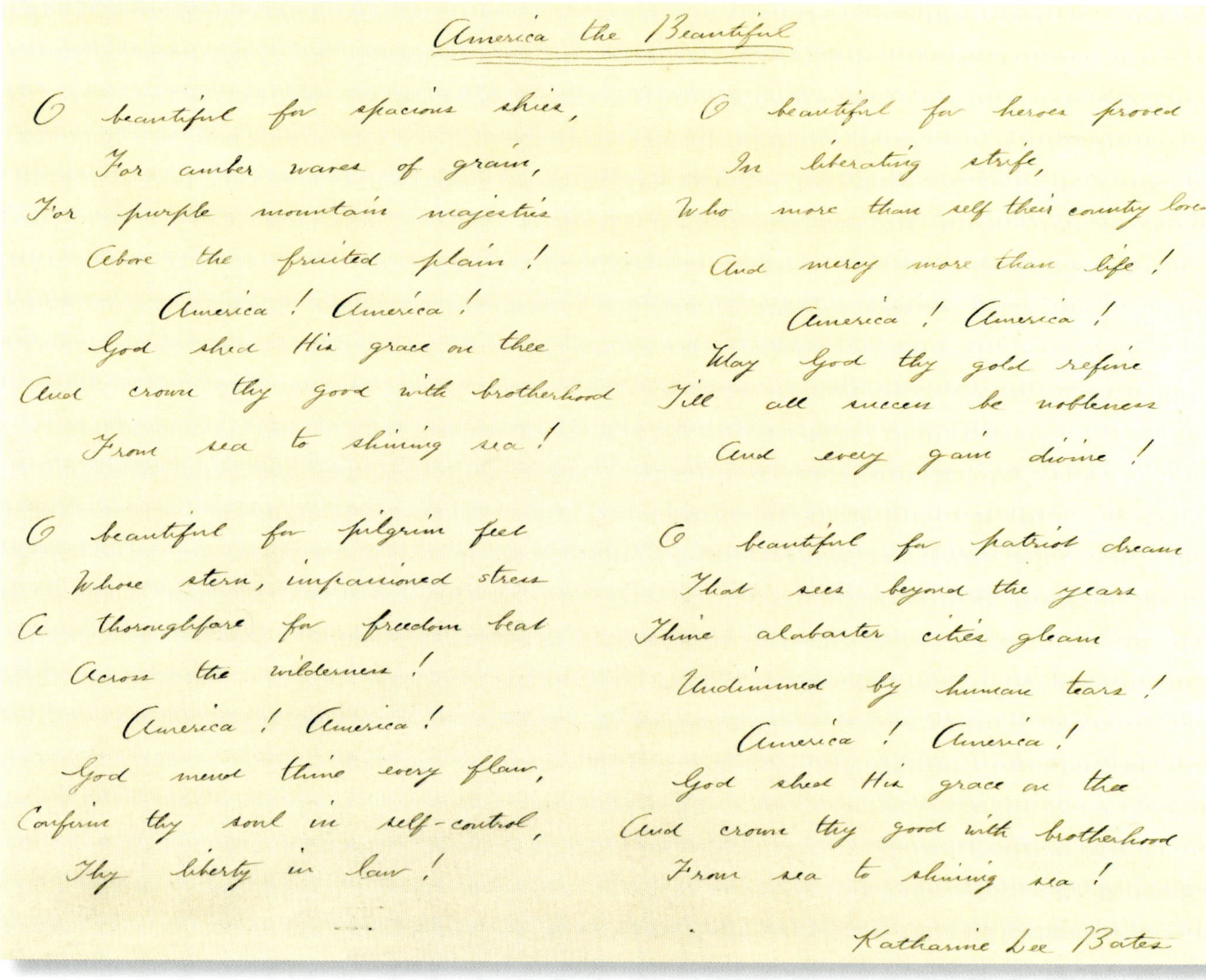

America the Beautiful

O beautiful for spacious skies,
For amber waves of grain,
For purple mountain majesties
Above the fruited plain!
America! America!
God shed His grace on thee
And crown thy good with brotherhood
From sea to shining sea!

O beautiful for pilgrim feet
Whose stern, impassioned stress
A thoroughfare for freedom beat
Across the wilderness!
America! America!
God mend thine every flaw,
Confirm thy soul in self-control,
Thy liberty in law!

O beautiful for heroes proved
In liberating strife,
Who more than self their country loved
And mercy more than life!
America! America!
May God thy gold refine
Till all success be nobleness
And every gain divine!

O beautiful for patriot dream
That sees beyond the years
Thine alabaster cities gleam
Undimmed by human tears!
America! America!
God shed His grace on thee
And crown thy good with brotherhood
From sea to shining sea!

Katharine Lee Bates

"America the Beautiful" handwritten by its author

and summoned his musical entourage to an unusual early morning meeting in his suite at the Las Vegas Hilton. "It was out of nowhere," recalled Ed Enoch, the lead singer for Elvis's back-up vocal group, The Stamps. "He asked for our input, and I was thinking about the Ray Charles version, and how his was the best. There was just nothing else to do. And I didn't say a word, but Elvis looked at me and said, 'Hey, Ed, get that silly notion out of your head.' So all I did was to simplify the chords." Enoch told me they wrote the arrangement that morning and performed it that night, December 2, 1975. The emotional rendition became a mainstay of Elvis's bicentennial concert tour, regularly bringing tens of thousands of people to their feet, hands over their hearts. "He was very patriotic," Enoch said, echoing the sentiments of many Elvis intimates. "He did it because he felt it. I remember seeing tears in his eyes that first night." And then he paid his former boss the supreme compliment. "He sang it with as much soul as a white man could give."

I am convinced Katharine Lee Bates would have approved. "There was nothing static about her," a friend said. "Always she was moving with the times." She even anticipated our move to globalization, telling one audience:

> One of the suggestions that was most insistently made in these later years was that I add a stanza to express international brotherhood. It has not seemed easy to do that, for although I long for world brotherhood and am among those who look forward eagerly to the day when the United States shall enter the League of Nations, yet the song is long enough already, and is written for one special thing. So the best suggestion I can make is that when you sing the first stanza, you think of 'From sea to shining sea' as applying from the Pacific to the Atlantic, around the other way, and all the states in between, and that will include all the nations and all the people from sea to shining sea.

She remained an undeniable star, plowing through mountains of daily mail and greeting a constant stream of visitors to her home in Wellesley. Besides family members and friends, there were workmen and diplomats and congressmen and former pupils, many bringing their sons and daughters, and plenty of autograph-seekers. "All of them came and went away with a strange light in their eyes as if her starlike spirit had left them twinkling, too," recalled a friend.

In 1925 Katharine Lee Bates retired from Wellesley's English department after forty years of service. She had outlived most of her intimates: her mother, her sister, and Katharine Coman, who died of breast cancer in 1915. But she continued to be surrounded by friends, family, and her animals. When her beloved collie, Sigurd, died, she wrote a book about him and then buried him beneath a plaque on the campus. She got another dog, Hamlet, and then a parrot named Polonius. Unwilling to cage the bird, she daily fed him toast and coffee and carried him from room to room on a tightly clutched twig.

Bates's house on Curve Street, Wellesley, Massachusetts

Katharine and Polonius

REPUBLICAN WOMEN DECLARE FOR DAVIS

Seven New Yorkers and Prof. Bates of Wellesley State Their Views.

To the end, the books that nourished her vigorous intellect lay stacked everywhere, on the tables, the shelves, the desk, the chairs, and the couch. Her great-niece Jane Grant remembers being admonished to "Ssh—lower your voice!" and put on her best behavior when she visited as a child. "I was told, 'Now go very quickly past Aunt Katharine's study, because she's very busy,'" Grant recalled. "She was an important person." An adult visitor at the time described her warm, curtained study with its Corona typewriter and mounds of books as "a restful, peaceful place…with an atmosphere which seems to whisper, 'Here are born lovely thoughts.'"

As her heart weakened and her writing waned, Katharine Lee Bates maintained her curiosity and her sense of humor. When she was given a car and driver to make traveling more comfortable, she named the auto "Abraham" and installed a guest book for passengers to sign. When Wellesley College celebrated its fiftieth year in 1925, she was asked about the length of the fashionable new skirts. She reportedly said, "if skirts today are too short, those of fifty years ago were certainly too long." And she continued to make news. When she decided to vote for the Democratic presidential candidate in 1924, the *New York Times* wrote an approving editorial and found her defection worthy of a headline.

Confined to her bed one winter night in 1929, she disobeyed her doctor's orders and stayed up to hear Admiral Byrd's exotic broadcast from Antarctica. "I am speechless before the miracle of radio," she later told a friend, "by which one man can speak to millions over so many miles of frozen silence, and make all of them feel like one family around a single hearthstone."

Bates in her study, 1916. A picture of Katharine Coman
is on the wall behind her

In the early morning of March 28, 1929, after a bout of pneumonia, Katharine Lee Bates died in her own bed at the age of 69.

"Earth became a lonelier and a colder place when her warmth and valor were withdrawn," said her colleague Vida Scudder. At the college memorial, where "America the Beautiful" was played, the eulogies added a sparkling grace note to her legacy, noting her "contagious chuckle," her "nimble wit," and her "rather curious combination of rebellion and loyalty."

All of which were evident posthumously. For her funeral, Bates had said, "I hope…they will not make speeches about me, but will perhaps read some of my poetry instead." They did both. For her burial, in the family plot in Falmouth, she had directed cremation and, anticipating her final victory in the battle of the bulge, mused over her ashes, "I like to think how light they'll be." The inscription she chose for her gravesite was one more wry commentary on her unanticipated renown: "I will sing unto the Lord a new song."

As for her earthly creation, it continues to resonate, unchanged in an America she might not always recognize, but one that pays homage to her.

In **Falmouth, Massachusetts,** a sign on the road informs visitors that this village was Bates's birthplace, and the two-and-a-half story white Colonial where she grew up is appropriately marked. Once a museum, it is now privately owned. At the nearby Falmouth Historical Society, a roomful of exhibits contains relics of Katie's imaginative childhood, including delightful stick-figure drawings and the will she solemnly wrote out before she was twelve, leaving "all my worldly possessions in the way of dolls and toys to Hattie L. Gifford [her best friend], with the wish that she will give them to poor indians." You can also see the 1981 postage stamps issued to honor "America the Beautiful," and a brilliant green feather that once adorned the parrot Polonius.

A few blocks away, a bigger-than-life statue of a slimmer-than-ever professor stands on the library lawn, just in front of Katharine Lee Bates Road. Visitors can also

Katharine's birthplace today

Nearby on Curve Street, an oval plaque marks Bates's house, which is privately owned.

Not all the milestones on her journey to fame are so well preserved.

The **Fitchburg Railroad** that transported her West was folded into other companies, and service to the West on that line ended many years ago. The trains passing through the Hoosac Tunnel today carry freight, not passengers.

Niagara Falls currently attracts some 12–14 million visitors a year, but they see less of the Falls than Katharine Lee Bates did in 1893, thanks to falling rocks and diversion for hydroelectric power. Still, some 600,000 gallons of water per second fall over the edge, continuing to produce what Bates called "colossal plumes of spray."

In **Chicago**, the World's Columbian Exposition closed, as scheduled, in October 1893. After months of neglect, fire demolished much of the White City. The only building still standing is part of the Museum of Science and Industry. The Ferris wheel was moved to St. Louis for another fair in 1904, then dynamited for scrap.

The wheat fields of **Kansas** remain a potent symbol of American abundance despite their dependence on federal subsidies and the widespread consolidation of family farms into corporations. In the 1990s, state automobile license plates bore the inscription "amber waves of grain."

Colorado Springs has grown into a city of nearly 350,000. The glittering new lures are not gold mines but high-tech industries, along with the military

ride to nearby Woods Hole on the Shining Sea bikeway. At the cemetery, a line of signs directs visitors to the family plot.

At **Wellesley College**, where the students are less cloistered but the campus quite as gorgeous as when she entered, both a residence hall and a professorship are named for Katharine Lee Bates. The students sing "America the Beautiful" at every graduation.

PIKES PEAK

and plentiful suburbs. The Antlers Hotel burned down in 1898 and was totally rebuilt—twice. In its latest reincarnation, a wall display outside the Katharine Lee Bates Suite commemorates the hotel's role in the saga of the song.

Colorado College still runs a summer school, but professors are rarely imported from the East. A small bust of Katharine Lee Bates sits in one of the main buildings.

Pikes Peak remains a thriving attraction, although the 750,000 people making the ascent each year come as tourists, not settlers. Early in the summer, I retraced Bates's trip to the summit to see for myself the "glorious scenery" that had inspired her poem. Instead of the circuitous, nineteen-mile mule-drawn carriage that transported her to the top in 1893, I rode the more direct cog railway, an hour-long climb along an eight-mile track that provides a wondrous view of changing landscapes, layered like one of those arrangements of colored sand in a bottle. From the base at Manitou Springs (already an impressive 6,570 feet high), we passed through a forest of tall pines and lively

pikespeakcam.com

11:43:04 AM

7:12:10 AM

7:17:01 AM

4:38:05 PM

5:31:42 PM

www.pikespeakcam.com

streams that gave way gradually to giant pink boulders and gray granite rocks. At 9,500 feet—halfway there—we saw ponderosa pines with reddish bark, and started chewing gum to halt the popping of our ears. At 12,000 feet we glimpsed yellow-bellied marmots (that's an animal, not a slur) and coal-black ravens. Then, above the treeline, Arctic tundra—with a scruff of green lichen and vast snowfields even in May.

Finally, we reached the top, 14,110 feet, where I fully appreciated the dizzying effects of the mighty mountain. I felt unaccustomedly light-headed in the thin atmosphere, even short of breath, but after a brief rest in the bustling Summit Lodge and many gulps of water, I regained enough stability to venture outside. There, in the crisp clear air (thirty degrees cooler than the balmy base), I gasped at a panorama every bit as spectacular as Katharine Lee Bates had described: a sky so near and open, I thought I could touch it; a montage of cliffs and peaks that reached up even higher. The mountains in the distance really did look purple. And despite a mantle of haze, I could still see clear to Kansas.

True, the ever-widening arc of housing developments creeping up the mountainsides have irrevocably marred the pristine wilderness. And you could make the

104. Summit of Pike's Peak, Colo.

Where the author relieved her Inspiration of America the Beautiful !

Katharine Lee Bates's notation on a contemporary postcard.

NO EXIT — © Andy Singer

OH SMOG-FILLED, AIRPLANE-CROWDED SKIES, GENETICALLY ENGINEERED **GRAIN**. DENUDED MOUNTAINS, MINING ROADS, AND AGRIBUSINESS **PLAINS**! AM-ER-I-CA, AM-ER-I-CA, GREED'S ALMOST DESTROYED **THEE**, AND TURNED THY WOODS TO CONSUMER GOODS AND OVERFISHED YOUR **SEAS**!

SINGER

But here's the point. What I saw from atop Pikes Peak is not the literal picture of America that Katharine Lee Bates painted back in 1893, because she wasn't being completely literal then, either. America the Beautiful existed largely in her mind's eye, a dream for future generations, a radiant vision of everything the country she loved could, and should, be. If you need visual proof, a video camera puts Pikes Peak on the Web during daylight hours. And a tangible reminder of her creative powers can be seen at the summit itself, a giant bronze tablet bearing the first two verses of "America the Beautiful." It was erected during the song's centennial in 1993. But you don't need to read the words to appreciate the spacious freedom we enjoy and the unlimited potential of the country that the song celebrates. Nor do you have to climb Pikes Peak to understand what Katharine Lee Bates saw. America itself is her most enduring monument of all.

The icon that inspired the melody has its own lasting appeal.

Coney Island has seen better days, and public housing now looms over much of the once-refined resort. The **excursion boats** were discontinued more than half a century ago. But hundreds of thousands of subway riders still flock to the beach each summer, for the waves, the hot dogs, and yes, the Ferris wheel. And the carpet of sand just beyond the boardwalk continues to entice, an ageless lure into the deep blue waters, which remain a shimmering muse for anyone's imagination.

case—as a *Washington Post* editorial did in 1989— that the big picture has changed drastically, "[w]ith acid rain and deregulated airlines filling our spacious skies, with our amber waves of grain coated in pesticides and supported by billions of dollars in farm subsidies, with the purple mountains denuded and the fruited plains rapidly being turned into malls."

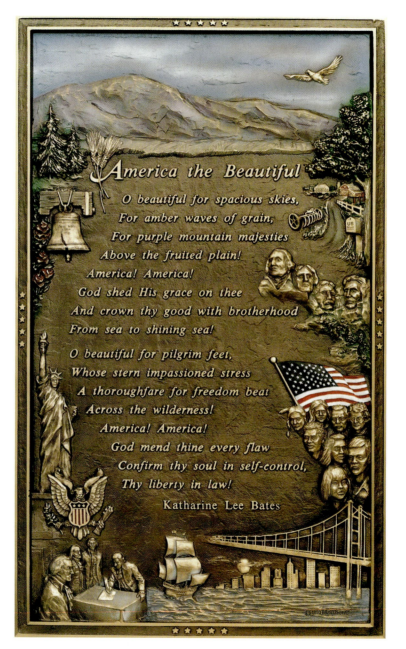

The plaque atop Pike's Peak

In **Newark,** all but one of Samuel Augustus Ward's residences have been razed for bigger buildings or parking lots. The yellow brick house in which he died still stands downtown, but it bears no plaque, no memory of the composer or his creation. His grave at Mount Pleasant Cemetery in Newark, a leafy park that became the final resting place for many of Newark's elite, is marked by a modest granite block next to that of his wife, Virginia. Just beyond are the tiny stones of two daughters who died in childhood.

At **Grace Episcopal Church**, a stately, English Gothic structure on Newark's aptly named Broad Street, a multiethnic inner city congregation has grown in recent years. A bronze plaque in the vestibule recounts the accomplishment of its former organist, the only such monument to his achievement. Grace Episcopal is likely one of the only churches in the nation that annually sings "O Mother Dear Jerusalem"—long gone from the hymnal—because, as the current organist James MacGregor, told me, "Every time I hear the tune sung with "America the Beautiful" I think, 'It's from here! It's right here!'"

The **Orpheus Club** still holds concerts twice a year, singing "America the Beautiful" at the beginning of each performance in tribute to Samuel Augustus Ward.

There is a living legacy as well.

Ward's great-granddaughter, Virginia Morrell, lives in the Caribbean with her family and cried when she told me that "America the Beautiful" was played at her wedding. Her grandson is named Samuel.

Katharine Lee Bates's great-niece, Jane Grant, lives in New England, and conceded in true Yankee

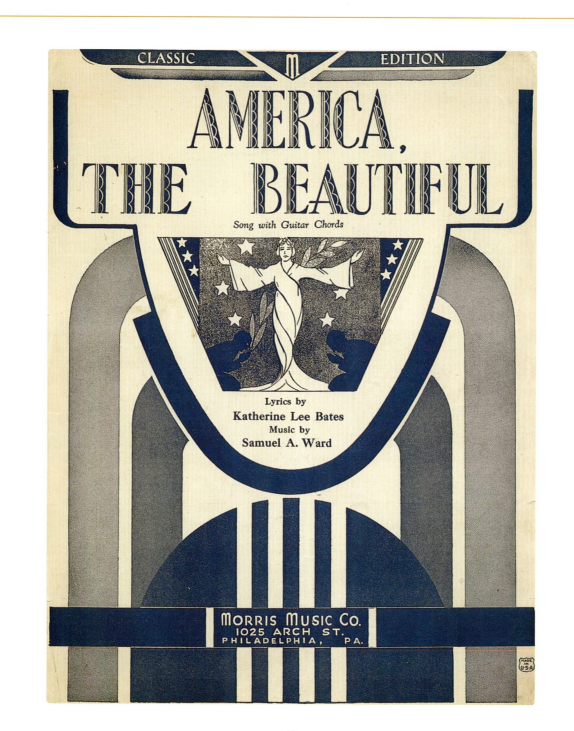

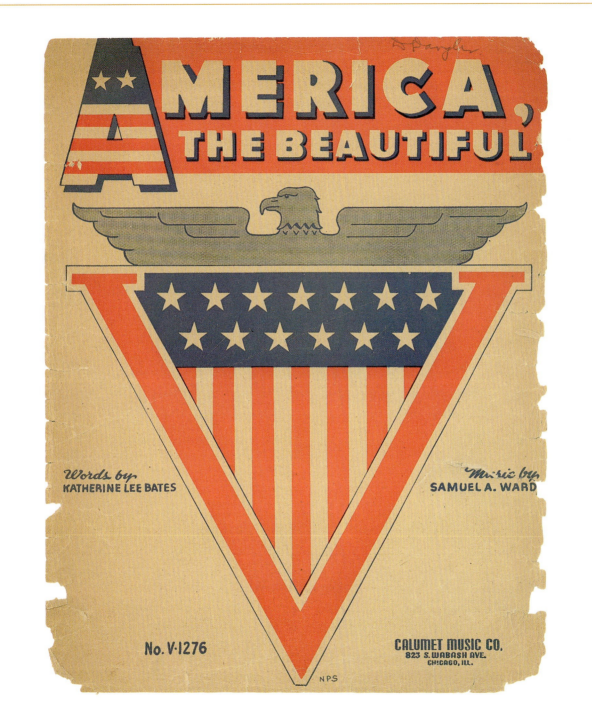

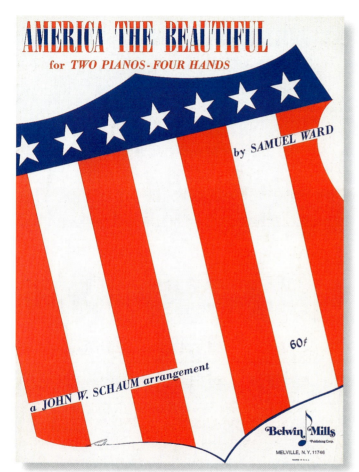

modesty that the song makes her feel "almost teary." Grant's granddaughter is named Katherine.

But that's about as much as these quietly proud families boast about their heritage. It seems to be an inherited trait. Jane Grant couldn't remember ever hearing "Aunt Katharine" talk about the song. "I think she was tired of all the fuss," she told me. Bates herself made that clear in a letter. She admitted only to a "sense of personal attachment" for a creation she called "so accidental and so simple…It has already yielded me far more honor than I ever dreamed of having." She elaborated ever so slightly: "I doubt if ever a bit of verse brought to the versifier so rich a reward in friendship, kindness and courtesy as this has brought to me." There was certainly no financial reward. Except for the $5 fee she received from *The Congregationalist* in 1895, Bates—like Samuel August Ward—received almost no money for "America the Beautiful." Both freely granted permission to use their works. For Bates, a poet whose income was largely dependent on her writings, her generosity of spirit was rooted in a concept as selfless as the song: She gave this one away—"my own slight gift to my country"—because she didn't believe she owned it, any more than she owned the purple mountains or the shining seas. "It belongs to all Americans whose feeling for America it expresses," she said. "I have come to see that I was its scribe rather than its author. Its singers are its true creators."

That probably gives the rest of us too much credit, but the author would allow no other interpretation. "It is not work to write a song: it is great joy," she said.

Which is exactly how it feels to sing it.

JUNE/JULY 1986 $2.75 $3.75 Canada

Sheet music
—STANDARD PIANO / GUITAR—
Magazine

America The Beautiful

Liberty ★ Acres Of Clams ★ Bonnie Blue Flag
Deep River ★ I Ride An Old Paint ★ Harrigan
Mademoiselle From Armentieres ★ The Girl I
Left Behind Me ★ Jeanie With The Light Brown
Hair ★ John Henry ★ Marie From Sunny Italy

ACKNOWLEDGMENTS

This book, like the song itself, has many roots. Here are some of them:

At Wellesley College, I am especially grateful to Wilma Slaight, whose meticulous and enthusiastic management of the Wellesley College Archives made my research there a constant delight. Thanks also to Jean Berry, and to President Diana Chapman Walsh for her encouragement.

The families of both Katharine Lee Bates and Samuel Augustus Ward generously responded to all my requests for help. Very special thanks to Jane Grant, Anne Grant Stanley, and Katherine Stanley for keeping the poet's flame burning. And deep gratitude to Virginia Morrell and Adam Morrell for keeping the musician's memories and mementos safe.

Many other helpful individuals gave openly of their time and information. In Falmouth, Massachusetts: Ann Sears at the Falmouth Historical Society and Robert Bidwell; in Newark, New Jersey: Charles Cummings of the Newark Public Library and James McGregor of Grace Episcopal Church; also, Grace-Ellen McCrann of the New Jersey Historical Society and Bill Gordon of the Newark *Star-Ledger*. In Colorado Springs: Edwina Foreman, Film Commissioner, and Todd A. Wilson of Colorado College; in Rochester, New York: Jack Handy and Jane Grant of Lake Avenue Baptist Church; in Nashville: LaVonne Gaw of Graceland and Ed Enoch.

Thanks also to two former members of Congress, Margaret Heckler and Andy Jacobs; to Nan Keohane, Mike Milewski of the University of Massachusetts-Amherst, Melinda S. Ullrich of the National Federation of Music Clubs, Hal Worthley of the Congregational Library, Carl P. Daw Jr. of the National Hymn Society, Martha Mitchell at Brown University, Don Singalewitch of the Orpheus Club, Lonn Taylor, Frank Tucker, Arnold Collins and Dr. Andrea Hinding of the YMCA, David Ritz, Melinda Ponder, Sandy Bates, and Steve Barnett.

To the singular Marvin Hamlisch, whose insights and energy both confirmed my own excitement and helped focus the story, a giant thank-you.

At PublicAffairs, I have enjoyed a welcome reunion with Peter Osnos and the wise guidance of my editor, Kate Darnton and managing editor, Robert Kimzey.

As usual, the book was buoyed by the incomparable agentry and friendship of Esther Newberg and by the knowing tolerance of my family and friends. Thank you all.

PHOTO CREDITS

SELECTED BIBLIOGRAPHY

Of the dozens of books and articles I consulted, these are the most relevant.

Badger, R. Reid. *The Great American Fair: The World's Columbian Exposition and American Culture*. Chicago: Nelson Hall, 1979.

Bates, Katharine Lee. *America the Beautiful and Other Poems*. New York: Thomas Y. Crowell, 1911.

——*An Autobiography in Brief*. Privately printed, 1930.

——*America the Dream*. New York: Thomas Y. Crowell, 1930.

——"How I Came to Write 'America the Beautiful,'" Privately printed, 1928.

——*Selected Poems of Katharine Lee Bates*, edited by Marion Pelton Guild. Boston and New York: Houghton Mifflin, 1930.

——Untitled essay for the *Boston Athenaeum*, 1918.

Brands, H. W. *The Reckless Decade: America in the 1890s*. New York: St. Martin's Press, 1995.

Burgess, Dorothy. *Dream and Deed*. Norman: University of Oklahoma Press, 1952.

Converse, Florence. *The Story of Wellesley*. Boston: Little, Brown and Company, 1915.

Glasscock, Jean, general editor, and Katharine C. Balderston, et al. *Wellesley College 1875–1975: A Century of Women*. Wellesley, Mass.: Wellesley College, 1975.

Guild, Marion Pelton. "A Practical Idealist: Katharine Lee Bates and Her Poems." *Zion's Herald*, May 6, 1931.

Horowitz, Helen Lefkowitz. *Alma Mater: Design and Experience in the Women's Colleges from Their Nineteenth-Century Beginnings to the 1930s*. New York: A. A. Knopf, 1984.

McFadden, E. L. "America's Great Peace Hymn." *The Etude*, December 1947.

Palmieri, Patricia Ann. *In Adamless Eden: The Community of Women Faculty at Wellesley*. New Haven and London: Yale University Press, 1995.

Prime, William Cowper. *O Mother, Dear Jerusalem: The Old Hymn, Its Origin and Genealogy*. Edited by William C. Prime. New York: A.D.F. Randolph, 1865.

Taylor, Lonn. *The Star-Spangled Banner: The Flag that Inspired the National Anthem*. New York: National Museum of American History, Smithsonian Institution in association with Harry N. Abrams, Inc., 2000.

Trachtenberg, Alan. *The Incorporation of America: Culture and Society in the Gilded Age*. New York: Hill and Wang, 1982.

Tucker, Frank H. "A Song Inspired." *Colorado Heritage*, Issue 3, 1989: 32.

White, Richard Grant. *National Hymns: How They Are Written and How They Are Not Written— A Lyric and National Study for the Times*. New York: Rudd & Carleton, 1861.

INDEX

A NOTE ABOUT THE AUTHOR

Lynn Sherr got hooked on "America the Beautiful" as a student at the all-women's Wellesley College, where students routinely substitute "sisterhood" for "brotherhood" when they sing the chorus. Wellesley was home to the song's author, Katharine Lee Bates, who taught English there for decades. It was also where Sherr honed her passion for writing. An award-winning journalist, she is the author of *Failure is Impossible: Susan B. Anthony In Her Own Words*, *Tall Blondes: A Book About Giraffes* and the co-author of ten editions of *The Woman's Calendar* and *Susan B. Anthony Slept Here: A Guide to American Women's Landmarks*.

Lynn Sherr's illustrious journalism career has included work at *Mademoiselle*, *Glamour*, *Vogue*, The Associated Press, WCBS-TV, PBS, and ABC News. She has written for *The New York Times*, *Saturday Review*, *Ms.*, and *O Magazine* among others. She is currently a correspondent for ABC News *20/20*. Television may be Sherr's best-known venue, but as she sat down to write the story of "America the Beautiful," she found herself doing something she'd never done professionally before: She was singing.

PublicAffairs is a new nonfiction publishing house and a tribute to the standards, values, and flair of three persons who have served as mentors to countless reporters, writers, editors, and book people of all kinds, including me.

I. F. Stone, proprietor of *I. F. Stone's Weekly*, combined a commitment to the First Amendment with entrepreneurial zeal and reporting skill and became one of the great independent journalists in American history. At the age of eighty, Izzy published *The Trial of Socrates*, which was a national bestseller. He wrote the book after he taught himself ancient Greek.

Benjamin C. Bradlee was for nearly thirty years the charismatic editorial leader of *The Washington Post*. It was Ben who gave the *Post* the range and courage to pursue such historic issues as Watergate. He supported his reporters with a tenacity that made them fearless, and it is no accident that so many became authors of influential, bestselling books.

Robert L. Bernstein, the chief executive of Random House for more than a quarter century, guided one of the nation's premier publishing houses. Bob was personally responsible for many books of political dissent and argument that challenged tyranny around the globe. He is also the founder and was the longtime chair of Human Rights Watch, one of the most respected human rights organizations in the world.

For fifty years, the banner of Public Affairs Press was carried by its owner, Morris B. Schnapper, who published Gandhi, Nasser, Toynbee, Truman, and about 1,500 other authors. In 1983 Schnapper was described by *The Washington Post* as "a redoubtable gadfly." His legacy will endure in the books to come.

Peter Osnos, Publisher

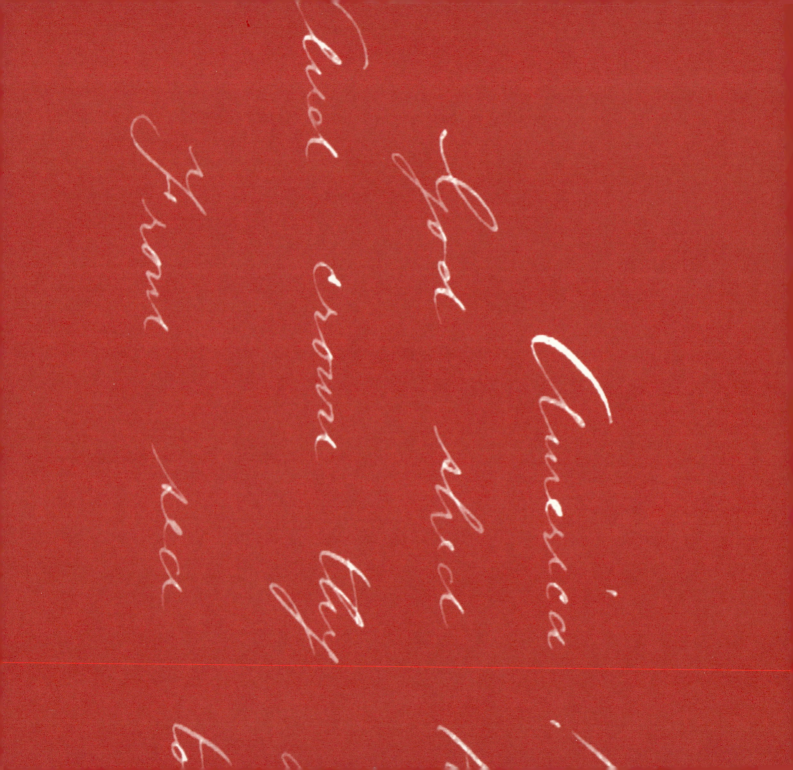